THE TWILIGHT OF STEAM

Great Photography from the Last Days of
Steam Locomotives in America

Photography by Robert A. Buck, George C. Corey, Gordon S. Crowell,
John Gruber, Fred Matthews, John E. Pickett, Gordon R. Roth,
Jim Shaughnessy, Richard Steinheimer, J. William Vigrass,
Philip A. Weibler, and Ron Wright

With text by BRIAN SOLOMON

Voyageur Press

To John Gruber, who is devoted to encouraging railway media.

CONTENTS

INTRODUCTION

FOR AMERICAN RAILROADS, the early 1950s was a time of rapid transition as colorful new diesels quickly displaced steam locomotives. The economics of diesel power were so compelling that once production models had been perfected, the writing was on the wall. Yet many observers often didn't see the writing until it was almost too late. Others were more astute and stayed ahead of the tide of dieselization, making photographs of the last of steam for posterity.

Aggressive postwar dieselization occurred faster than most railroaders imagined it would. After World War II, the big roads anticipated complete dieselization by 1965; yet by the mid-1950s, steam power already was well on its way to total oblivion. General Motors' Electro-Motive Division was churning out standardized diesel "units" as fast as it could. In 1947, author Franklin M. Reck cooed in his book, *On Time*—a promotional account of the Electro-Motive story—that the builder was completing "four to six locomotives a day!" While this was good news for GM and the railroads that sought to benefit from the greater efficiency of modern power, it spelled the end of an era for dyed-in-the-wool steam enthusiasts.

For them, the loss of steam represented the loss of individual character and a quelling of the railroad drama. Steam locomotives were imbued with personality; they seemed to live and breathe like enormous mechanical leviathans. Where every railroad had operated its own distinctive steam locomotives, diesels by contrast were largely standard models.

A flood of new locomotives, combined with changing traffic patterns, enabled some medium-sized railroads to complete the transition much earlier than expected. New York, Susquehanna & Western effectively dieselized by the end of World War II. In 1949, the recently created Gulf, Mobile & Ohio, which had never bought a new steam locomotive, boasted total dieselization.

Railroad traffic surges fueled by the Korean War kept steam rolling, but as that conflict receded and diesels continued to arrive en masse, steam locomotives were sidelined rapidly. Often whole divisions were converted to diesel operation just as quickly as crews could be trained to operate and maintain the new equipment. While the transition occurred over a number of years on some roads, on others, the once occasional diesel became the norm overnight. For casual observers, it seemed as if steam disappeared suddenly; one day there was a lonesome whistle in the valley, the next the drone of an air horn. The old engines that had worked the railroad for decades might be seen parked along the side of a yard where they'd rot, white-lined and rusting with their headlights, bells, and rods removed. Their final trip came when a shiny new Alco or EMD hood-unit towed them away for scrap. Some were unceremoniously cut up on the property.

As early as 1947, Boston & Maine reported that seventy percent of its traffic was diesel-hauled. Some of its newest and most modern steam engines, the handsome Mountain types, were largely off the property before steam ended. Although a decade passed before B&M was entirely dieselized, many of the engines that finished out the steam era were antique 2-6-0s from the early part of the century. Those old Moguls survived in Boston suburban service, where they worked light runs, notably on the Central Mass route. By contrast, mainline tonnage was hauled behind EMD F-Units and Alco road switchers.

By the early 1950s, steam had been totally vanquished from several big eastern lines, including Lackawanna, New Haven, and New York Central's Boston & Albany affiliate. With each passing month, photographers seeking mainline steam action found fewer options. Even railroads that still had steam on the roster were just holding engines in reserve in case of seasonal traffic surges, or they had relegated steam to far corners of their systems where they worked specialized traffic.

Despite the diesel onslaught, fodder remained for the steam enthusiast. In the late 1940s, even as General Motors was drowning the market, a few railroads continued to order new steam power. To avoid antagonizing their coal customers, while continuing to take advantage of relatively cheap local fuel, a few coal roads held off buying diesels longer than most. Baltimore & Ohio, Norfolk & Western, and Pennsylvania railroads were notable among the eastern carriers that continued to work their big steam in heavy mainline freight service years after EMD and Alco diesels were the norm elsewhere. Through the mid-1950s, visitors to the N&W were virtually assured a spectacular steam show. Other surviving steam lines required more patience. While steam was still out there working, finding it was another matter.

During the transition, diesels and steam often worked the same main lines. Certainly some photographers were happy to photograph whatever came along; for them, finding steam was an added bonus. But the serious lens-men were entirely focused on preserving the old order on film and saw diesels as interlopers unworthy of photographs.

PLATE 1 (PREVIOUS) A Duluth, Missabe & Iron Range 2-10-4 Texas type moves a heavy iron ore train in northern Minnesota. *John E. Pickett*

PLATE 2 Gainesville, Georgia, engine house 17, 1953. *Gordon S. Crowell*

CHAPTER ONE

NEW ENGLAND

NEW ENGLAND OFFERED a distinctive railway environment. Because many of its lines had been built early in the course of U.S. railroading, they followed sinuous alignments adhering to the contours of the land, winding along rivers and through villages and old mill complexes. The smaller scale of New England railroading tended to result in shorter, lighter trains hauled by more conservatively sized engines than those in mainline use elsewhere in America.

New England's railroads were local to the region. Even New York Central's Boston & Albany affiliate retained considerable independence in the steam era, with equipment lettered for the line. In southern New England, the New Haven and the Boston & Maine were dominant, while northern New England states were served by colorful regional networks: Rutland, Maine Central, and Bangor & Aroostook. Canadian railroads had a notable presence. Canadian National Railway's Central Vermont and Grand Trunk lines operated steam power that bore a strong family resemblance to Canadian National's own engines. Canadian Pacific served northern Vermont via its Quebec Central, and its transcontinental main line bisected northern Maine. It was on this latter route, in the lightly populated north woods, that the last mainline steam in New England operated in 1960.

Rutland was a regional steam holdout, having ordered four new Mountain types from Alco after World War II. These had short lives, as anyone at the time with a clear picture of motive power trends could have predicted: Rutland's new 4-8-2s were delivered just as nearby Boston

& Albany was replacing its Berkshires with new Alco freight diesels.

While Boston & Albany completed dieselization ahead of national trends, other New England lines continued to operate vintage mainline steam well into the 1950s. Among these was Central National's Central Vermont Railway running a north-south alignment from the Canadian border near St. Albans, Vermont, to the port of New London, Connecticut, via Palmer, Massachusetts. While not really a mountainous railway, Central Vermont had its fair share of steep grades on its hill-and-dale profile.

REMEMBERING THE CENTRAL VERMONT'S DAYS OF STEAM

Bob Buck of Warren, Massachusetts, documented steam on his favorite lines and continued to make photographs well into the diesel era. In his teenage years, Bob often traveled with his friend and fellow photographer, Warren St. George, also of Warren. Buck grew up in sight of the Boston & Albany; from a very young age he watched trains pass on the main line. He was familiar with the Central Vermont, its engines, and its men, and on a clear, quiet morning he could hear the distant sounds of Central Vermont engines climbing south from Palmer through Monson several miles away, the haunting sound of the engine's exhaust and whistle often just barely audible over the wind.

In his teenage years, to reach Palmer, Bob would buy a ticket on a Boston & Albany local passenger train, catch a ride with the local freight, or rely on the generosity

of relatives to drive him. He experienced the railroad both from the ground and from the cabs of engines. By 1946, he was old enough to drive himself to Palmer and made regular visits to watch Boston & Albany steam and to visit his friends on the Central Vermont.

"The CV people were still using the telegraph in 1946–1947," Bob recalls. "There was a Southern Division dispatcher in those days named Jim C. Pierce who worked second trick [night shift]. The agents in Palmer were Bob Brittan on first trick and John Merton on second trick.

"We'd get Jim going, but he needed a straight man to set him up. 'Oh Jim, what is the title of that book you're writing?' He'd answer, *The Smartest Man on the Central Vermont and How I Got That Way.*'"

By the mid-1950s, mainline steam was done on the New Haven and the Boston & Albany, and was largely relegated to Boston suburban runs on the Boston & Maine. However, Central Vermont was still assigning its trusty 2-8-0s to freights. For the most part, these old engines had worked Southern Division freights since before World War I. By contrast, Central Vermont's "big" 2-10-4 Texas types (the smallest 2-10-4s built in North America and New England's biggest engines) worked freight north of Brattleboro only because they were too heavy for the Millers Falls high bridge. But Canadian National's Fairbanks-Morse C-Liners (opposed-piston diesels) were appearing on through freight; it was obvious that the days of steam were coming to a close.

Bob Buck hoped for one last mainline steam cab ride, but his options narrowed quickly as more and more diesels showed up, borrowed from parent Canadian

National. "If I was going to get a chance to ride steam on CV, the time was going to be soon," he recalls. "John Merton suggested that I write to Superintendent Frank Weber, known as 'Breezy Webber,' to get permission to ride southbound CV train No. 430. John said I'd ride south and he'd arrange to get me back north again. I wrote to Webber and signed a release to keep everyone out of trouble, but for a while nothing happened. Then one Sunday, CV's Art Richardson gave me a call.

"'They're running steam,' he said, 'I think you'd better go.'

"I said to Art, 'I'll give John Merton a call and see if he can give me a ride back from New London.'

"'Look, he's away. Just go! Maybe you can get a ride on the northbound. Or you can take a bus to Springfield. If all else fails, you have your thumb!'

"I followed Richardson's advice. We had engineers Hawkes and Shepard, and I rode from the yard in Palmer to New London. It was a tough pull up State Line Hill through Monson, but they made it. Once over the hill, they did what CV's crews did best. And what did they do best, you ask? Exceed the speed limit!

"CV's employee's timetable limited freights to thirty miles per hour. I estimated we were in the high fifties dropping down Lebanon Hill; however, engineer Hawkes defended this action, saying, 'If you make a good run, you'll get home in time for supper.'

"He got in in time for supper that night. And hors d'oeuvres too!"

PLATE 4 Boston & Albany Hudson No. 618 leads train 554 east of Warren, Massachusetts, summer 1950. *Robert A. Buck*

PLATE 5 New York Central No. 3006 leads the westward New England Wolverine at Riverside, Massachusetts, March 25, 1950. *George C. Corey*

PLATE 6 Boston & Albany No. 1436 leads an eastward symbol freight at the Warren Crossovers, Warren, Massachusetts, 1947. *Robert A. Buck*

PLATE 7 Boston & Albany eastbound train 10 meets train 49 at Pittsfield, Massachusetts, winter 1947. *Robert A. Buck*

PLATE 8 The Boston section of Rutland's Green Mountain Flyer eastbound at Cuttingsville, Vermont, 1951. *John E. Pickett*

PLATE 9 In 1950, Rutland Railroad was working steam on through passenger services. The modern lightweight coach, seen here in the railroad's namesake Vermont city, seems incongruous with the steam locomotive hailing it. *John E. Pickett*

PLATE 10 Boston & Maine No. 1493 marches west from a station stop at South Sudbury, Massachusetts, 1955. *George C. Corey*

PLATE 11 Central Vermont Nos. 468 and 462 lead southward freight 430 at Palmer, Massachusetts, May 16, 1953. *Robert A. Buck*

PLATE 12 Central Vermont extra 466 south climbs Stateline Hill as it crosses Route 32 in South Monson, Massachusetts, October 13, 1946. *Robert A. Buck*

PLATE 14 Fireman's view of Central Vermont freight south of Norwich, Connecticut. *Robert A. Buck*

PLATE 13 Fireman's view from a Central Vermont southbound freight climbing through Monson, Massachusetts, on its way to the summit of Stateline Hill. *Robert A. Buck*

PLATE 15 Canadian Pacific's eastward Scoot crosses the bridge at Onawa, Maine, en route to Brownville Junction, April 9, 1955. *Jim Shaughnessy*

CHAPTER TWO
THE NORTHEAST

AS STEAM LOCOMOTIVES were phased out of regular service, dedicated steam photographers grew more focused in their pursuit of their subject. As operations wound down, there were ever fewer steam strongholds.

Sometimes it was the image that escaped the camera that stuck with a photographer and became the muse that kept him going. This memory would keep him searching for images of steam as the technology waned. And every steam photographer knew that time was running out—every moment of every day trackside counted.

JOHN PICKETT, STEAM HUNTER

John Pickett was fortunate to grow up in Canajoharie, New York, just across the Mohawk River from New York Central's four-track main line at Palentine Bridge. He started making photos before the onslaught of diesel power, and his early New York Central photos were exposed with 616 Kodak Monitor. Later he bought a National Graflex with a relatively fast Bausch & Lomb f3.5 lens and 1/500th of a second top shutter speed. Next came a Series B Graflex with a top shutter speed of 1/1000th of a second. "I bought my film locally in Canajoharie," John recalls. "Back then you could buy film anywhere. I'd use 616 roll film and process it at home with Kodak MQ developer."

Through travels with his family, John also witnessed steam on the Boston & Maine and the New York, Ontario & Western, among other lines. His early acquaintance with the New York Central and other lines led to his later pursuit of steam. Through the 1950s, John traveled far and wide across North America, capturing steam in its final decade. He estimated that he spent an entire month following steam in 1952 and at least two weeks in 1953.

Although there were still a lot of steam locomotives working, John couldn't spend every waking hour trackside. Among other necessary distractions were studies at the University of Pennsylvania, followed by a stint in the U.S. Army. He finished this service in April 1955 and moved back to Philadelphia, where he worked for United Airlines. Having a good job gave him resources for his railroad photography. On weekends and days off, he continued to seek out steam, looking both on his doorstep and farther afoot.

When he was a student at Penn in the late 1940s and early 1950s, John often traveled with fellow photographers Fred Kern and Bert Pennypacker. They would make one- and two-day jaunts in Fred's car into anthracite coal country. "I should have been back at Penn studying," John recalls. But the lure of steam distracted him.

To find out where steam was working, John sought the advice of fellow photographers when traveling. He also found railroaders helpful. "Back then there were lots of railroad people around that you could speak to," he says. "There were manned stations all over the place. I'd go find the agent and ask what was going on. Most of them were friendly, although one time we had a run-in with a guy up on the Milwaukee Road in Montana who wasn't very helpful. When I asked him about a freight that was expected, he replied gruffly, 'I'm having my lunch and I won't talk to you.' Well, it didn't matter, we followed the tracks and found the train anyway!"

As late as 1955, the Pennsylvania Railroad and the Reading Company still worked classic Pacific types on Atlantic City trains over their jointly run Seashore Lines. A timetable and a little patience would reward him with the sight of steam power leaving Philadelphia terminals for the Jersey shore. Both railroads used a short section of PRR's electrified main line to reach the Delaware River bridge, where trains crossed into New Jersey.

For some pictures, John stood on Philadelphia's Girard Avenue bridge, which faced PRR's multiple-arch span over the Schuylkill, to catch aged Pacifics marching out of town in time-honored tradition. For this traffic PRR assigned its highly regarded K4s Pacific types ("s" for *superheated*). These big-boiler machines featured PRR's characteristic boxy Belpaire fireboxes and trappings common to its road engines. Steam was most certainly the exception at this location, not because of diesels, but because PRR's multitrack wired main line was populated by a constant parade of electric trains. The railroad's famous Brunswick green Raymond Loewy–styled GG1 electrics led many of these. As Philadelphia Transportation Company trolleys hummed along Girard Avenue, John would wait for the telltale sight of steam and bark of exhaust that announced approaching steam locomotives. Except for the wires on the bridge, the photos he exposed were not that different than scenes made there thirty years earlier.

In fall 1955, John made an excursion to western Pennsylvania seeking steam on the Baltimore & Ohio. "I had a tip from my good friend, Bert Pennypacker, that B&O was still running its World War II–era EM-1s on the main line," he explains. Now *here* was an opportunity. B&O's EM-1s were no ordinary steam locomotives; they were modern 2-8-8-4 Yellowstone-type simple articulateds. During the war, B&O had wanted to buy more Electro-Motive FT diesels, but the War Production Board refused, so B&O turned to Baldwin for these powerful articulated types.

PLATE 16 A Pennsylvania Railroad K4s Pacific leads an Atlantic City train across the Schuylkill River in Philadelphia, circa 1955. *John E. Pickett*

John was keen to catch these machines in action. "They were exceptionally handsome engines," he says. "In my opinion, they are what Delaware & Hudson and Western Maryland *should* have ordered instead of 4-6-6-4 Challengers. The EM-1 would have given those roads better service."

Connellsville, Pennsylvania, was a long way from Philadelphia. "I had my maroon 1952 Mercury hardtop, which I drove to Connellsville on two-lane roads," John says. "I arrived there in the afternoon and made some nice engine pictures. I stayed overnight and made a few more photos the next morning. The highlight was finding one of the EM-1s working a big eastbound freight heading toward Sand Patch.

"Gosh, that was great. I followed it for three hours, staying with it until dusk and making photos all along the way. Somewhere along the line the train stopped to pick up a 2-10-2 helper for the climb to Sand Patch."

By dusk, John had reached Meyersdale where B&O's main line snaked under Western Maryland's massive tower-supported trestle. Here he made a stunning sequence of photos showing the head-end EM-1 and the 2-10-2 working at the back. "I had a great time," he says, "but it sure was a long drive back to Philadelphia."

THROUGH THE LENS OF GORDON ROBERT ROTH

Gordon Roth grew up in Short Hills, New Jersey, and was bitten by the railway bug very early when his father would bring him trackside on the Delaware, Lackawanna & Western to see the "steamies," including the railroad's flagship *Lackawanna Limited*, race through town. On weekends during World War II they would visit Central Railroad of New Jersey's Garwood Station. In 1942, Gordon began using a Brownie to make photos on these excursions while his father enjoyed the Sunday paper. During the war, paranoia about photography reigned, often resulting in encounters with the local police. Undeterred, he remained an active railway photographer and continued to produce stellar steam work.

Among those who influenced Gordon's railway work was Don Furler, who not only introduced him to a fraternity of accomplished enthusiast photographers, including Robert Collins and Walter Lucas, but impressed Gordon with his successful application of 5x7 in Speed Graphic for railway photography. Gordon felt that this format was better for railway images, as it was proportionally longer than the 4x5 film used by many serious railway photographers. Gordon worked predominantly with Kodak Super Panchro Press Type B sheet film as well as Kodak Royal Pan. Later, he was impressed with Ilford's HP3, promoted as the "fastest film available" and rated at 250 ASA. He also experimented with Ansco Super Hypan.

After a stint as photographer for the U.S. Navy's Pacific Fleet, Gordon pursued a career in commercial photography, which led him to Rochester Institute of Technology, where he studied from 1948 to 1950. Later, he worked as a photographer at Kodak, among other jobs. While in Rochester, Gordon served as president of the Rochester Chapter of the National Railway Historical Society between 1950 and 1955, which put him in touch with many other active and budding railway enthusiasts. Among them was Ron Wright, who was still very young, but budding with enthusiasm, and Jim Shaughnessy (both Wright and Shaughnessy are also featured in this book). Gordon regularly attended what he calls "railroad photography get-togethers," some hosted by Michael Koch in Scarsdale, New York, and attended by Collins, Furler, Shaughnessy, and other well-known steam photographers like Phil Ronfor and Bob Malinoski. Through this fraternity, photographers shared their experiences, railway operating information, and imaging techniques.

JIM SHAUGHNESSY, IMAGE MAKER

Jim Shaughnessy's byline is undoubtedly one of the most familiar names in this book. Not only are Jim's photos some of the finest of the late steam era, but he was unusually prolific, as well, traveling across the North

American continent to document the rapidly changing railway scene.

Jim grew up in Troy, New York, a secondary railway hub across the Hudson River from Albany. He began photographing in his teenage years after World War II and was fortunate to have the support of his family during the formative years of his railway enthusiasm. His early photographs featured railways close to home, including the Boston & Maine, Delaware & Hudson, New York Central, and (his favorite) the Rutland, all of which served the Albany area.

Jim was part of various railway-enthusiast social circles and traveled with a number of other photographers over the years. Among them were John Pickett, with whom he has shared a friendship for more than six decades, and the late Dr. Philip Hastings.

From the beginning, Jim was interested in more than just locomotives, and his distinctive style is best described as "environmental." "I tried to capture the locomotives in a scene," he explains. "But to a degree my images should be self-explanatory." His broader interest allowed him to make a more comprehensive portrait of American railways during the crucial steam-to-diesel transition. He didn't exclude new diesels from his scenes and often made images of steam and diesel working side by side. Yet, "Diesels took some getting used to," he says. "They were certainly more colorful, but they didn't have the drama of steam."

Jim's open-minded approach kept him trackside long after steam locomotives finished; where some steam-era photographers effectively ended their work at the close of steam operations, or decided to pursue steam to the ends of the earth, Jim has continued to document American railways to the present day, regardless of the motive power.

From the mid-1950s through the mid-1960s, it seemed that Jim was here, there, and everywhere. From Quebec to Mexico and uncounted places in between, Jim was out day and night, making photographs. And it's in this last area that his work excelled. While many photographers made the most of daylight, then settled in for a good meal and a night's rest, Jim would head out after dinner to make some his most memorable images by blending natural light with flashbulbs.

Today, we might wonder what sorts of arrangements were necessary to make photographs at night in an active industrial environment, but in the 1950s a more relaxed attitude prevailed. "Some places like Cheyenne [Wyoming] and Conneaut [Ohio], you could write ahead," Jim explained. But more often than not, he would just show up with his cameras, tripods, and flashes. He'd approach railroaders as necessary to make his images, and often included them in the pictures. "Your demeanor had a lot to do with how you got on," he says. "If you behaved well, generally there were no problems [making photos] in yards and facilities."

Although Jim's voracious appetite for image-making produced a wide portfolio of railroads, one area of his photography that stands out is the photographs he made of Pennsylvania Railroad's Elmira Branch toward the end of steam. Jim learned through "the railfan grapevine" that PRR was still running steam on this route in the mid-1950s. "It was pretty well known that steam had concentrated remaining engines on the Elmira Branch," he says. Where other photographers despaired at the difficulties of photographing heavy trains working northward (and thus against the light), a frustrating environment for conventional engine pictures, Jim's environmental approach produced a stunning record of late-era applications of big steam at work side by side with diesels and in bucolic mountainous settings.

"On one trip," he recalls, "I traveled to Canandaigua, New York, where Phil Hastings was living to fulfill an obligation with the VA [Veteran's Administration]." Over the course of just a couple of days, Jim and Phil made dozens of splendid images of Pennsylvania Railroad steam in its final years of heavy work. If you knew no better, it would be easy to assume that months of photography were required to produce this portfolio.

PLATE 17
Pennsylvania Railroad No. 4521 L1s simmers at East Altoona Yard, April 28, 1957. *Ron Wright*

PLATE 18 New York Central No. 2748 leads a westward freight under a signal bridge decked with upper-quadrant semaphores at Palatine Bridge, New York, March 29, 1948. *John E. Pickett*

PLATE 19 Reading Company No. 217 departs Pottsville, Pennsylvania, October 16, 1949. *John E. Pickett*

PLATE 20 Reading Company No. 3002 leads a heavy freight west of Mahanoy Junction, Pennsylvania, May 1950. *John E. Pickett*

PLATE 21 Baltimore & Ohio No. 3140 pauses at a rural station near Galeton, Pennsylvania, on the former Buffalo & Susquehanna route, circa 1948. *Gordon R. Roth*

PLATE 22 Baltimore & Ohio No. 7615 leads an eastward freight into a curve on its Pittsburgh-to-Cumberland main line east of Connellsville (probably near Confluence, Pennsylvania), autumn 1955. *John E. Pickett*

PLATE 23 Baltimore & Ohio No. 7615 approaches Meyersdale, Pennsylvania, autumn 1955. *John E. Pickett*

PLATE 24 Baltimore & Ohio No. 6201 works behind a caboose as a helper while approaching Meyersdale, 1955. *John E. Pickett*

PLATE 25 A Delaware & Hudson freight led by No. 1523 ascends the Erie Railroad's grade south toward Scranton at Starrucca, Pennsylvania, late 1940s. *Gordon R. Roth*

PLATE 26 A second Challenger works as helper at the back of the same southward freight (previous). *Gordon R. Roth*

PLATE 28 An eastward Erie Railroad passenger train departs Newark, New Jersey, on the Newark Branch, February 8, 1947. *Richard H. Young, Solomon collection*

PLATE 27 Delaware & Hudson No. 1533 works toward Ararat Summit as it passes the famous curve at Thompson, Pennsylvania, March 1947. *Gordon R. Roth*

PLATE 29 Erie Railroad No. 3393 works west with a through freight at Jamestown, New York, October 13, 1946. *Richard H. Young, Solomon collection*

PLATE 30 Pennsylvania Railroad's East Altoona shop goat peaks out of the roundhouse, April 28, 1957.
Ron Wright

PLATE 31 Pennsylvania Railroad Class L1s Mikado No. 533, East Altoona, Pennsylvania, April 28, 1957.
Ron Wright

PLATE 32 Pennsylvania Railroad No. 6851 passes Newton Hamilton, Pennsylvania, September 13, 1951. *John E. Pickett*

PLATE 33
No. 6753 works
westbound with
a long freight on
the Middle Division
between Marysville
and Duncannon,
Pennsylvania,
October 4, 1955.
John E. Pickett

PLATE 34 Two Pennsylvania Railroad Hippos thunder eastward with an ore train east of Northumberland, Pennsylvania, summer 1955. *John E. Pickett*

PLATE 35 A Pennsy operator is ready to hoop up orders to a passing freight on the Elmira Branch near Troy, Pennsylvania, May 1957. *Jim Shaughnessy*

PLATE 36 A Pennsylvania Railroad I1s Decapod labors with a northward freight on the Elmira Branch, May 1957. *Jim Shaughnessy*

PLATE 37 A Pennsy M1a 4-8-2 passes splendid rural scenery at the "MAX" block limit (location of a passing siding) on the Elmira Branch in north-central Pennsylvania, May 1957. *Jim Shaughnessy*

PLATE 38 Ralston, Pennsylvania, May 1957. For a time, regeared Pennsylvania Railroad passenger-service Alco PAs worked on the Elmira Branch in helper service alongside I1s 2-10-0s and M1 4-8-2s. *Jim Shaughnessy*

PLATE 40 A northward Pennsylvania Railroad Decapod pounds across a gravel grade crossing near South Troy, Pennsylvania, May 1957. *Jim Shaughnessy*

PLATE 39 A blown-out cylinder disabled a Pennsy Decapod working as a
rear-end helper between Troy, Pennsylvania, and the New York state line. The
railroad sent a pair of new Alco RS-11 diesels to the rescue. *Jim Shaughnessy*

PLATE 42 East Broad Top No. 15 leads a coal train from Mount Union, Pennsylvania, south of Rockhill Furnace (near Orbisonia), November 3, 1953. *Gordon S. Crowell*

PLATE 41 Pennsylvania Railroad crewmen gaze idly at their locomotives at Watkins Glen, New York, August 20, 1956. *Jim Shaughnessy*

MANY STEAM PHOTOGRAPHERS treat the Nickel Plate Road with reverence. While a lot of lines were rapidly dumping the fires on steam, Nickel Plate kept the flame alight, continuing to order new steam power through the late 1940s. Yet, it wasn't just Nickel Plate's decision to stay with steam that made it the source of admiration. The railroad's classy style and fast operations garnered attention, as well. Also, it was an underdog, and one that appeared to be trying to outrun its competition.

Nickel Plate ran a tight ship. Unlike the big trunk lines, with their multiple-track main lines, Nickel Plate was largely a single-track outfit. But it made up for its lack of heavy infrastructure with tight scheduling and fast running. Also, it was an intermodal pioneer and one of the few railroads to run piggyback trailers behind steam.

Its late-era steam was among the finest too. Best known were its Berkshires, many of them Lima products (built at Lima, Ohio, a small industrial city served by Nickel Plate). Unlike the early ponderous Berkshires that slugged it out on long drags in their namesake mountains, Nickel Plate's Berks had high drivers and were built for speed across relatively level territory between Buffalo, Cleveland, and Chicago. (Level here is a relative term; Nickel Plate's line was hardly a billiard table. Yet, where Boston & Albany's Berks were built to ascend a continuous grade of more than 1.5 percent on one of the most sinuous mainline mountain crossings in North America, the Nickel Plate was characterized by rolling hogbacks and relatively tangent track in open territory.)

Nickel Plate Road was the working name for the New York, Chicago & St. Louis Railroad. In the 1920s, it had been core property of the Van Sweringen brothers' transportation empire. In those times it shared an affiliation with Chesapeake & Ohio and Erie railroads, among other lines. After the breakup of the Van Sweringen properties, Nickel Plate retained historic connections with the Wheeling & Lake Erie.

The Vans, as the brothers were commonly known, had envisioned melding their various railroads into a super trunk line that would vie for traffic with the Pennsy, New York Central, and Baltimore & Ohio. While the merger was never allowed, the Van Sweringen railroads benefited from a unified motive power policy under the direction of an Advisory Mechanical Committee that procured the best standard designs for the different railroads. Nickel Plate Berks were refined by years of working with "superpower" designs, and its last classes of 2-8-4s are considered among Lima's finest locomotives. (Lima originated the 2-8-4 design for the Boston & Albany in the mid-1920s.) The last of the type was Nickel Plate's No. 779. Sadly, Nickel Plate's most modern steam worked for less than a decade.

For a few years, when its handsome 2-8-4s were outpacing New York Central diesels on their respective lines, Nickel Plate seemed to buck the trend. The wheels of progress eventually caught up, however. The raw economics of the situation were unsustainable, and it was just a matter of time before a tide of diesels flooded Nickel Plate's ranks.

TEENAGE FASCINATION WITH THE NICKEL PLATE

Ron Wright was a teenager in the mid-1950s. By the time he was old enough to travel on his own, steam was done in his hometown of Rochester, New York. To find it, he would travel west to Buffalo and beyond, where engines were still working on the Nickel Plate Road.

In those days, long-distance phone calls were expensive and railroad magazines offered limited coverage of local operations. How did a young enthusiast find steam? "I had a relative in Buffalo who was a railfan and he tipped me off," Wright recalls. "'There's still steam coming into Buffalo.' Yet, I didn't really become aware of the Nickel Plate until 1955. In October, I had been invited into the cab of a diesel switcher working at Winton Road in Rochester, and the fireman told me of a steam graveyard at Gardenville in Buffalo. I didn't know where that was, so I wrote it down and asked my parents to drive me there. After we went to Gardenville, we stopped at the South Park Bridge in Buffalo." Here, Ron saw live steam on the Nickel Plate, an event that inspired a dozen or so solo trips to photograph Nickel Plate steam in action.

Steam-era railroaders were often sympathetic to the plight of a young enthusiast with a camera. On occasion, Ron was able to hitch rides on switchers after a long day of photography in the Buffalo area.

"I made two trips to photograph steam in Westfield," Ron explains. "Nickel Plate was pretty busy here, and on September 29, 1956, I saw six to eight freights."

He also made repeated visits to Dunkirk. "I'd hang out in AK Tower, where Nickel Plate had a diamond crossing with a New York Central branch [to Titusville, Pennsylvania]," he says. "They were always good to me there. It was cold in the winter standing around waiting for freights [but warm inside the tower]."

PLATE 43 Nickel Plate Road No. 779 works a freight near Fredonia, New York, St. Patrick's Day 1957. *Jim Shaughnessy*

PLATE 44 Nickel Plate Road No. 288 switches at Buffalo, New York, July 19, 1957. *Ron Wright*

PLATE 46 Nickel Plate Road No. 775 at Ridge Road in Lackawanna, New York, October 20, 1956. *Ron Wright*

PLATE 45 Nickel Plate Road Nos. 278 and 748 under steam at Buffalo, New York, October 14, 1956. *Ron Wright*

PLATE 47 Lackawanna, New York. Nickel Plate Road No. 303 seen from the fireman's side of a Buffalo Creek Alco switcher, August 11, 1957. *Ron Wright*

PLATE 48 Nickel Plate Road No. 779 seen from the window of a New York Central passenger train west of Buffalo near Athol Springs, New York, November 23, 1957. *Ron Wright*

PLATE 49 Nickel Plate Road No. 746 works eastbound at Dunkirk, New York, November 23, 1957. *Ron Wright*

PLATE 50 Nickel Plate Road No. 170 leads a
passenger train in central Ohio, circa 1956.
J, William Viqrass

PLATE 51 Nickel Plate Road No. 737 works a train of refrigerator cars at Mayfield Road in Cleveland, Ohio, April 1955. *J. William Vigrass*

PLATE 53 Nickel Plate Road locomotive shops, Conneaut, Ohio, 1957. *Jim Shaughnessy*

PLATE 52 Nickel Plate Road eastward freight, west of Buffalo, New York, March 8, 1958. *Jim Shaughnessy*

PLATE 54 Nickel Plate Road No. 778 working west meets New York Central F7s near Conneaut, Ohio, March 1957. *Jim Shaughnessy*

ROANOKE, VIRGINIA, WAS THE LAST great mecca for heavy mainline steam in the United States. This was the heart of Norfolk & Western's operations. Here, N&W's Roanoke Shops built new steam locomotives until 1953, several years after commercial builders delivered their last domestic steam. It wasn't until 1954 that N&W finally ordered diesels; its steam continued to work in revenue service for another half-dozen years.

Not only did N&W remain an all-steam operation for several years after many other railroads began conversion to diesels, but it was also a busy and well-groomed line. Ballast was trimmed, track was immaculate, locomotives were exceptionally well maintained, *and* the railroad had a lot of heavy freight traffic, all while hosting several handsome named streamlined passenger trains. Here coal trains were the rule. These were heavy and required N&W's biggest, most powerful engines: the famous Y-class Mallets.

John Pickett organized a pilgrimage to N&W in April 1956 that rewarded him with many memorable images and experiences. "I'd arranged for four days off from United [Airlines], and I drove all the way to Roanoke," he says. "It wasn't all hardship. I drove west to Harrisburg then down to Hagerstown. From there I followed the Shenandoah Valley, making photos of N&W's line along the way.

"I had a permit from N&W to go on the property. At Roanoke I had the opportunity to sit in the cab of N&W's coal-fired turbine electric, the *Jawn Henry*. What I remember about it was that there was a fine layer of coal dust on everything in the cab. I was impressed with this engine. It was a *big*, big machine!"

Photographing N&W was easy compared to other roads. The railroad kept the brush down along the right of way. "Even in 1956 this was a true steam stronghold," John says. "I don't recall seeing any diesels anywhere, not even as switchers in the yard.

"I had a timetable for the passenger trains, and these were still all steam-hauled too. I caught the freight trains when they came along, and I never waited long. The N&W was a busy road; there was always something happening!"

Compared with some roads, N&W had relatively few classes of mainline steam power. Long-distance passenger trains were led by streamlined J-class 4-8-4s and a few K-class 4-8-2s (some of which were streamlined similarly to the Js); the Y-class Mallets and A-class simple articulateds moved road freights. The Mallets were the biggest engines on the line, the last true compound locomotives built in America, and the last of their breed working a main line. But they weren't John's favorites. "I liked the As the best," he explains. "They were graceful, attractive, and well-proportioned engines. They were beautiful machines, I thought. Although the Ys were big, they just didn't have the style of the As."

Despite his affinity for the As and his good fortune to have witnessed N&W steam in action, more than fifty-five years after his visits, John has some regrets. "I dearly wished that N&W had saved one of the Y6s for themselves," he laments. "You know, to run, like they did with the J [No. 611] and A [No. 1218]. Sure, I know there's an N&W Y6 in the museum at St. Louis, and the Illinois Railway Museum has a Y3, but it would have been great to see one of N&W's Y6 under steam again. It's a real pity."

Although N&W was popular with other photographers, most notably O. Winston Link, who made his famous night images in the final years of N&W steam, John notes that in spring 1956, "I didn't travel with other photographers or see anyone else around." There were grades to the east and west of the yards at Roanoke. "I worked both sides. I'd been here back in 1954, and then I'd found a place to stay trackside just west of Roanoke. Today, you'd call it a bed and breakfast, but back then it was just a guesthouse, and only cost six dollars a night. It was great. You'd look out the window right at the stack of a passing locomotive."

N&W steam was the big show, but John kept his eyes open. "I also photographed the Virginian, which was still operating its big electrics," he says. This insight paid off. "Some of my pictures were featured in Bill Middleton's *When the Steam Railroads Electrified*." John snapped some of the Virginian's big Fairbanks-Morse diesels too.

John made good use of his time and photographed from many scenic locations. "The Js really marched along with passengers, but the Ys weren't slow. They came along at pretty good speed too," he recalls.

Not everything was easy. On the last afternoon of John's April 1956 visit, he had to change a tire trackside. "There was a heavy layer of cinders along the right-of-way. I'd jacked up my car," he says. "But then the jack shifted in the cinders and the car awkwardly settled down." John wondered if he'd make it back to work the next day, but he didn't give up. "I ended up digging a hole under the car for the jack and eventually got the tire changed. I don't recall missing any trains as this was going on."

For John, 1956 was really the last good year for steam. After that, even on the N&W, diesels were taking over. "They really dieselized quickly," he says. "By 1960 it was all over."

While the N&W was the last "big" steam show, it was by no means the only attraction in coal regions. Although less photographed, the Chesapeake & Ohio and Louisville & Nashville were big steam operators until the mid-1950s, as were a host of smaller lesser-known lines.

PLATE 55 A Norfolk & Western local sails across a plate-girder trestle in the Shenandoah Valley, April 1956. *John F. Pickett*

PLATES 56 AND 57
A Norfolk & Western
Class A works
westbound near Elllston,
Virginia, April 18, 1956.
John E. Pickett

PLATE 59 Norfolk & Western No. 134 leads the eastward *Powhatan Arrow* at Glenvar, Virginia, April 21, 1956. *John E. Pickett*

PLATE 61 Norfolk & Western No. 2160 and a second Y-class Mallet work east with a coal train, 1956. *John E. Pickett*

PLATE 60 Norfolk & Western No. 1237 works a manifest freight, circa 1956. *John E. Pickett*

PLATE 62 Norfolk & Western
Y-class Mallets thunder upgrade
with a coal train in 1956.
John E. Pickett

PLATE 63 N&W No. 1218 rolls in the opposite direction with a water tender on the railroad's busy double-track main line. *John F. Pickett*

PLATE 64 Norfolk & Western No. 608 leans into a curve with a passenger train, 1956. *John E. Pickett*

PLATE 65 Norfolk & Western No. 613 with a passenger train, April 1956. *John E. Pickett*

PLATE 66 Norfolk & Western No. 610 departs Roanoke with the westbound *Cavalier,* April 1956. *John E. Pickett*

PLATE 67 The engineer of Chesapeake & Ohio No. 1624 gingerly works the throttle, May 1956. *Philip A. Weibler*

PLATE 68 Chesapeake & Ohio No. 1624 labors with 160 cars in tow, May 1956. *Philip A. Weibler*

PLATE 69 Chesapeake & Ohio No. 1624 pauses by the Thurmond, West Virginia, station with eastward coal loads, May 1956. *Philip A. Weibler*

PLATE 70 Baltimore & Ohio local near Buckhannon, West Virginia, July 1, 1956. *Jim Shaughnessy*

PLATE 71 Emory River Railroad's lone locomotive, No. 6940, leads a coal drag near Gobey, Tennessee, October 19, 1953. *Gordon S. Crowell*

PLATE 72 Louisville & Nashville No. 1895 leads a westward freight near Baxter, Kentucky, October 20, 1953. *Gordon S. Crowell*

THE MIDWEST

THE AMERICAN MIDWEST is a crossroads of commerce. It has long been a place where East meets West, a place where railroad lines radiate from industrial and commercial centers to connect at major gateways in Chicago, Kansas City, and St. Louis. The great variety of railroads, junctions, main lines, secondary lines, branches, yards, and terminals made it a fascinating place to watch and photograph trains. As railroads switched from steam to diesel, the Midwest was one of the first regions to experience diesel power. But it also hosted some of the last big steam operations.

The Burlington Route experienced one of the longest steam-to-diesel transitions of any American line. It effectively introduced the diesel streamliner to America in 1934 with its famous Budd-built, Electro-Motive-powered stainless-steel *Zephyr*. Over the next two decades it continued to order diesels for all applications, but it also operated mainline steam through the mid-1950s, several years after many of its neighbors were fully dieselized.

For the steam-hungry photographer, the Midwest presented opportunity but sometimes frustration as well. As diesels invaded, railroads often stored steam sooner than expected. Photographers hoping to find engines at work might arrive at a known steam oasis only to find long lines of cold engines without work to do. Weeks later, a traffic rush might find these same old engines back under steam for one last glorious pull before being allocated for scrap. Among the lines that attracted

photographers in these last years were the Illinois Central, Burlington, and Duluth, Missabe & Iron Range, which not only operated steam very late, but also kept big engines busy on the main line.

GROWING UP ALONG MIDWESTERN LINES

Phil Weibler spent his teenage years within earshot of midwestern steam, first near Chicago & North Western's main line at West Chicago, and later at Quincy, Illinois, near the Burlington. He began trying to capture steam on film in 1952 at age fourteen using a Baby Brownie Special to expose 127-size negatives. Like steam photographers everywhere, he faced a race against time. "I started taking good pictures in 1953," he says. "Every time you turned around another steam operation had finished."

For the teenage steam enthusiast, time and money needed to be budgeted carefully. Phil recalled that for him thirty-five cents was the key figure—his weekly allowance. This could buy just one roll of film or process one roll of film. It also was the cover price for *Trains* magazine. In 1953, he upgraded to a better camera, a 2¼ x 3¼ Speed Graphic. The camera was complex and difficult to use at first, requiring film packs or cut film holders. A simple modification allowed the use of a roll film holder that used readily available 120 film.

Phil's earliest photography was along the C&NW main line near his home at North Kirk Road between

West Chicago and Geneva. He hadn't yet earned a driver's license, so he used his bicycle to reach the tracks. A ticket from Geneva to West Chicago cost, you guessed it, thirty-five cents. "I could put my bicycle in the baggage car," he says. "When I got to West Chicago, I'd ride over to the roundhouse then ride home."

In summer 1952, when his family relocated to Quincy, Phil began to focus on the Burlington and the Wabash. The sounds of steam remained strong in his memories of Quincy. "We rented a house on the northwest side of town," he remembers. "At night Burlington worked a local freight with a pair of matched 2-8-2s. These had a fascinating sound. They'd get into synch with each other [while climbing the grade] then drift out again." Later, Phil made photos of Burlington's trains climbing out of the Mississippi Valley to the tops of the bluffs.

Burlington steam impressed Phil. "C&NW's engines were absolutely filthy. Sometimes they were so dirty the engineer would have to clean off the cab side to read the engine number," Phil says. "But Burlington's engines at Quincy were glossy black with graphite smokeboxes and gold lettering. These seemed absolutely spotless."

Phil's interest in railroads led to his career. He began college at Virginia Tech in a co-op engineering program that had him working March to May of 1956 as a special apprentice at the Norfolk & Western's Shaffer's Crossing roundhouse in Roanoke, Virginia. He transferred to the University of Illinois at Champaign that fall and met up

PLATE 73 Chicago & North Western No. 629 leads state-of-the-art bi-level suburban cars at North Western Station in Chicago, 1955. *Philip A. Weibler*

with Bruce Meyer and Parker Lamb, well-experienced railroad photographers. The trio made several trips together in 1958. Incidentally, the Illinois campus was also home to Jim Boyd (later editor of *Railfan* magazine and author of many books), Don Ball (author of several notable railroad books), and Ted Rose (later a *Trains* graphic artist, best known for his watercolors of evocative railway scenes).

"J. Parker Lamb, Bruce, and I often traveled together," Phil recalls. "People have accused me of 'borrowing' Bruce's negatives, but in fact I was standing right next to him."

Graduating in 1960, Phil went right to work for the Rock Island as a switchman in Chicago. "Returning from the army in 1963, I went to work in the System Mechanical Department, first at Silvis Shops and later at Kansas City," he says. "In 1972, I went to the Chicago & North Western as a training officer. Several years later I went into engine service, qualifying as a locomotive engineer in 1975. It all came full circle when I fired a job for Oscar Foster. I'd known Oscar when he was the fireman on Number 13 back in the early '50s."

Wabash was an unusual railroad. It connected gateways at Buffalo, Chicago, St. Louis, Omaha, and Kansas City. It was also one of the few American lines that operated main lines east and west of Chicago. From the late 1920s, the Pennsylvania Railroad controlled it, but this had little visual effect on its locomotive policy. It dieselized rapidly after World War II, and its steam was largely finished by 1953. One peculiar exception was its branch line from Bluffs, Illinois, (on the Decatur–Kansas City mainline) to Keokuk, Iowa. An old bridge at Meredosia, Illinois, could not take the weight of diesels, so sixty-year-old 2-6-0 Moguls continued to work the line.

Wabash was less photographed than other lines in its territory. Compared with Nickel Plate and Burlington, Wabash photos are rare. Yet, some photographers made the pilgrimage to catch Wabash's Moguls, not simply because these were its last steam, but because they were so ancient, a throwback to another time.

For Phil Weibler, the Wabash moguls were an opportunity to catch some really interesting locomotives on film. While he photographed Wabash steam switchers in Quincy, the allure of the Moguls sent him on a quest in 1954. Finding out about the details of specific operations wasn't easy, but Phil recalls, "I had correspondence with guys here and there, and you'd get secondhand information."

Bluffs was home to the Moguls, but Wabash was a tenant of the Burlington at Keokuk. "I went to the roundhouse where Burlington had a hostler who took care of Wabash's Moguls," Phil explained. "Sometimes Wabash would double-head them on trains. A 2-6-0 arriving at Keokuk would have its fire cleaned, be coaled, watered, and turned, and then sent home. A canteen [auxiliary water car] trailed the tender when the train left town."

The Official Guide of the Railways had a two-inch listing for the Bevier & Southern Railroad Company. This obscure fifteen-and-a-half-mile Missouri short line probably would have gone unnoticed if it wasn't for its relatively late steam operation. The company connected with Burlington at its namesake, and Phil made the trip to see it. "In 1958, Bruce Meyer and I were snooping around looking at short lines," he says. "I'd gone through the *Official Guide* and typed up postcards which read, 'Are you still operating steam? Where are the best locations?' That's how we found the B&S.

"[The B&S] leased a Burlington 2-8-2, which they worked hard and let get filthy dirty. Their own engines, however, were kept in immaculate condition. They basically forwarded coal loads to the Burlington, and Burlington took care of all the paperwork."

What was really unusual about the B&S was that it had train radios in the cabs of its steam locomotives. This was before most of the big railroads had adopted radio for train communications.

PLATE 74 A Burlington local freight running from Quincy to Galesburg nears the top of the bluff on the climb out of Quincy, Illinois, December 1953. *Philip A. Weibler*

PLATE 75 Illinois Central locomotives in the unnatural light of the Paducah, Kentucky, shops, September 1, 1957. *Jim Shaughnessy*

PLATE 76 Chicago & North Western R-1 4-6-0 No. 1376 switches freight at Geneva, Illinois, 1952. *Philip A. Weibler*

PLATE 77 Chicago & North Western No. 395 takes water at Madison, Wisconsin, 1954. *Philip A. Weibler*

PLATE 78 A selection of steam power at Chicago's North Western Station, including one of two Pacifics fitted with streamlined shrouds, 1955. *Philip A. Weibler*

PLATE 79 Chicago & North Western's West Chicago roundhouse and engine facilities, viewed from the Wilson Avenue bridge, circa 1952. *Bob Meiborg photo, Philip A. Weibler collection*

PLATE 80 Chicago & North Western No. 3031 at North Western Station in Chicago, 1952. *Philip A. Weibler*

PLATE 81 Burlington No. 5634 thunders across the Milwaukee Road/
Illinois Central diamonds at Mendota, Illinois, late 1950s. *John E. Pickett*

PLATE 82 Burlington No. 5141 at Quincy, Illinois, 1953. *Philip A. Weibler*

PLATE 83 A Burlington Texas type leads a coal train at Abingdon, Illinois, 1955. *Philip A. Weibler*

PLATE 84 Wabash No. 546 as it works industrial trackage at Quincy, Illinois, 1952. *Philip A. Weibler*

PLATE 85 Wabash No. 587 is serviced by a Burlington hostler at Keokuk, Iowa, June 1954. *Philip A. Weibler*

PLATE 86 Wabash No. 587
at Keokuk, Iowa, June 1954.
Philip A. Weibler

PLATE 87 A Bevier & Southern locomotive under steam at the company shops, Bevier, Missouri, 1958. *Philip A. Weibler*

PLATE 88 Duluth & Northeastern 2-8-0 No. 28 hits a rural road crossing in northern Minnesota, September 21, 1957. *John E. Pickett*

PLATE 90 (overleaf) Duluth, Missabe & Iron Range No. 221 pulls loaded ore jennies to port at Lake Superior, June 1953. *John E. Pickett*

THE DENVER & RIO GRANDE WESTERN had a firm policy of not allowing riders on its narrow-gauge freight trains in southwestern Colorado and northern New Mexico. But as service was nearing an end in 1967, *Trains* magazine wanted a photo story and I received the assignment. I had been a regular contributor since 1960.

David P. Morgan, the longtime editor, knew that Gus Aydelott, D&RGW president, would find a way to make this happen, so Morgan sent a request to the railroad's headquarters in Denver. Morgan quietly maintained a friendship with many railroad officials, and Aydelott was among them.

So Aydelott arranged to have me listed as an employee of a contractor doing business with the railroad. Narrow-gauge service was infrequent, so I got a few weeks' advance notice to prepare and drive from Madison,

Wisconsin, to Alamosa, Colorado, with two Nikon F camera bodies and lenses.

The train orders leaving Alamosa on August 28 were for "Extra 498 and 493 West," which became the name of the article. The D&RGW added a caboose and sent two people to watch over me: Trainmaster-Roadmaster H. V. Meek from Alamosa and Ed Rose, advertising manager from Denver. But they did not restrict me in any way, and I was able to exercise my style of photography: close-up pictures of people at work at the front and back of the train.

I got unusual and unique views between Alamosa and Chama, where I had chosen to spend the two days. At 10,015 feet above sea level, Cumbres Pass was, as it is today, impressive. Later, I photographed the shops in Alamosa and the Farmington branch from the highway. Soon after my trip, on September 18, the D&RGW

filed for abandonment of these freight lines, effective the following year. Morgan spoke for all of us: "And so the narrow gauge gets in the blood and will not get out" (*Trains*, October 1969).

What was missing was an interview with the train crew. It was with great joy that in 2013, I located Gayle Cunningham, a retired railroader I had photographed. In 1967, he was a locomotive engineer who did not have enough seniority to hold an engineer's job, so he was the fireman on No. 493. He told me how much he liked working on the narrow gauge. "Oh, I loved it. Yes I did," he says. "I knew it was a little dangerous because of the old track and the old trains, but when you are that young, you don't pay any attention to danger."

Was it hard work shoveling coal on the steep grades? "Well, no," he says. "I grew up on a farm shoveling grain all the time. A scoop shovel was nothing to me."

PLATE 91 A Denver & Rio Grande Western narrow-gauge freight with a rear-end helper cut in ahead of the caboose negotiates the Garfield Wye on the Monarch Branch, August 15, 1952. *John E. Pickett*

PLATE 92 A crew waters a Denver & Rio Grande Western 2-8-2 Mikado. *Philip A. Weibler*

PLATE 93 Rio Grande narrow-gauge Mikados work a Monarch Branch quarry train crossing the standard gauge Royal Gorge route at Salida, Colorado, to take water, June 22, 1955. *Jim Shaughnessy*

PLATE 94 Denver & Rio Grande Western No. 493 pulls a freight across a low pile trestle on the Farmington Branch, 1967. *John Gruber*

PLATE 95 Denver & Rio Grande Western No. 497 is seen through the door of the Alamosa, Colorado, shops, 1967. *John Gruber*

PLATE 96 Rio Grande Mikados work fore and aft on a short but heavy tank train climbing Cumbres Pass, 1963. *John Gruber*

PLATE 97 Enthusiasts take in the grandeur of a Rio Grande freight that requires Mikados at both ends to ascend difficult grades in the Rockies, 1967. *John Gruber*

PLATE 98 Rio Grande freight near the summit of Cumbres Pass, Colorado, 1967. *John Gruber*

CHAPTER SEVEN
THE WEST

RAILWAYS IN THE AMERICAN WEST have an undeniable lure, with crystal-blue skies, wide-open panoramas, and rugged mountain grades comprising the perfect ingredients for stunning images. Compared with the dense overlapping networks in the East and Midwest, routes have always been sparse in the West. Yet, the West's main lines have served as heavily traveled steel lifelines, while its branch lines have been lightly traveled.

A combination of difficult grades and the need to move large trains over great distances encouraged western lines to develop some of the largest, most powerful, and most distinctive steam locomotives in the world. Among the best remembered were Union Pacific's twenty-five massive 4-8-8-4 Big Boys, built in the 1940s for service between Cheyenne, Wyoming, and Ogden, Utah, and often deemed the world's largest engines.

There were other distinctions to Western steam, notably the early and widespread adoption of oil-fired engines as a reaction to the paucity of regional coal reserves and the cheap availability of local oil. The Santa Fe Railway pioneered oil-fired engines in the early twentieth century. Yet, a dearth of coal wasn't the only operating problem it faced. Its heavily traveled east-west trunk crossed the parched deserts of Southern California, Arizona, and New Mexico. To keep its boilers full, the railroad had to transport tens of thousands of gallons of water daily, a condition that made the Santa Fe an early candidate for dieselization. Consequently, Santa Fe was the first of the western lines to buy large fleets of Electro-Motive's pioneering road freight diesel, known as the FT, and during World War II effectively dieselized operations along its driest main lines. On other lines, however, it continued to operate big steam into the 1950s, often alongside EMD F-Units and other diesels.

The most distinctive of western oil-burners were Southern Pacific's cab-forward articulateds developed before World War I as a means of using massive Mallet compounds in the difficult operating environment on Donner Pass, where miles of high-elevation line enclosed by tunnels and snow sheds made conventionally configured Mallets unworkable because of the danger of crew asphyxiation from exhaust fumes. Later, as compounding fell out of favor, SP adapted its cab-forward concept into a powerful, simple articulated locomotive.

SP was the dominant railroad in the far West. At one time its lines reached in every direction from the Golden State. As late as World War II, it had been America's third-largest passenger railroad. Its streamlined *Daylight* passenger trains were deemed some of the most beautiful trains in the world. The orange, red, black, and silver Lima 4-8-4s developed in the 1930s were still working in the early 1950s, as were many of its cab-forwards. These distinctive engines were a big draw for photographers, who traveled from the East Coast to witness them in action.

SP's operations were gradually dieselized over the dozen years after World War II. As diesels took over, remaining steam was concentrated into late-era strongholds, resulting in photographers focusing on the San Francisco–San Jose peninsula "Commutes" (suburban passenger trains), where SP cascaded road locomotives as diesels assumed more important long-distance runs. This was the last place to find SP's Lima 4-8-4s working hard in mainline service. More obscure was the banishment of cab-forwards to the remote Modoc Line running from Fernley, Nevada, across the barren northeast corner of California to Klamath Falls, Oregon. Here, having been bumped from work over Donner Pass,

relatively modern oil-burning articulateds replaced their older cousins in heavy freight service.

Some of the last regular steam operations in the West were on logging railways in the foothills of the Sierra Nevada and the forests of the Pacific Northwest. After mainline steam had finished, photographers focused on these relatively obscure locations.

Fred Matthews and Richard Steinheimer lived in California during the colorful steam-to-diesel transition. Matthews began photographing SP steam locomotives in the late 1940s. "About 1947 it became obvious that steam was on its way out," he recalled. "It was just a matter of when. Initially, Matthews' photography was a family exercise; later he was a member of the University of California Railfan Club, which had the benefit of railway author George Hilton as their faculty advisor.

Matthews worked with a Kodak 620 Vigilant, a folding compact roll-film camera with a pronounced bellows arrangement that made eight 2¼ x 3¼ images per roll. He started using black-and-white Kodak Verichrome film and later Kodak's improved Verichrome Pan (for panchromatic), which more accurately interpreted color scenes into black-and-white images. In later years, he upgraded to a 4 x 5 Speed Graphic. "This was sharp but a burden to use," he says. "I had to remember which film holders I'd exposed and I had not." As might be imagined, double-exposing film wasn't a prized exercise among railway photographers.

"I also had Zeiss Super Ikonta [another variety of folding-roll camera]," Matthews adds. "I dropped that on a platform at Pontiac, Michigan, and that was the end of that."

PLATE 99 San Luis Central No. 1 with a single tank car and a long line of refrigerator cars near Monte Vista, Colorado, October 3, 1953. *Gordon S. Crowell*

PLATES 100 AND 101 Union Pacific No. 4018 exits the Hermosa Tunnel on Wyoming's Sherman Hill, August 20, 1957. *Both Jim Shaughnessy*

PLATE 102 Union Pacific Nos. 4017 and 4024 rest at the Laramie, Wyoming, engine terminal, August 20, 1957. *Jim Shaughnessy*

PLATE 103 Union Pacific No. 3967 marches eastbound with a mile of freight in tow across the plains of eastern Wyoming, July 1, 1955. *John E. Pickett*

PLATE 104 Great Western Railway of Colorado No. 90 works a trainload of sugar beets, late 1950s. *John E. Pickett*

PLATE 106 Santa Fe Railways Baldwin-built No. 3753 sits alongside Electro-Motive EA diesels at San Diego, August 1949. *Richard Steinheimer*

PLATE 105 A mix of Santa Fe Railway steam and diesel power hauls an eastward freight at Melrose, New Mexico, August 31, 1952. *John E. Pickett*

PLATE 107 Northern Pacific No. 1375 marches across a fill near Richland, Washington, June 23, 1955. *John E. Pickett*

PLATE 108 National Railways of Mexico Nos. 269 and 260 lead
a northward freight across Route 115 between Cuautla and
Ozumba, St. Patrick's Day 1961. *John E. Pickett*

PLATE 109 West Side Lumber Company No. 10 near Tuolumne, California, circa 1957. *Richard Steinheimer*

PLATE 111 Southern Pacific cab-forward No. 4213 leads a freight on the Modoc Line, spring 1955. *John E. Pickett*

PLATE 110 Crew with Southern Pacific cab-forward articulated
steam locomotive No. 4191 at Fernley, Nevada. *Richard Steinheimer*

PLATE 112 Southern Pacific No. 4329 under steam at the Oakland Pier, December 1949. *Fred Matthews*

PLATE 113 Southern Pacific *Morning Daylight* train 98, led by No. 4455, blasts out of the tunnel at Bayshore, California, August 24, 1952. *John E. Pickett*

PLATE 115 Southern Pacific's Cal-Stanford football special at First and Broadway in Jack London Square, Oakland, California, November 1947. *Fred Matthews*

PLATE 114 Southern Pacific No. 4444 leads train 133 at Seventh and Townsend streets in San Francisco, Christmas Eve 1956. *Fred Matthews*

PLATE 117 Steam at Dunsmuir, California, December 28, 1951. *Fred Matthews*

PLATE 116 View from the Dutch door on Southern Pacific's Los Angeles–bound *Morning Daylight* near San Luis Obispo on the Coast Line, August 10, 1953. *Robert A. Buck*

PLATE 118 Southern Pacific No. 4274 at Colton Yard, California, early 1950s. *Richard Steinheimer*

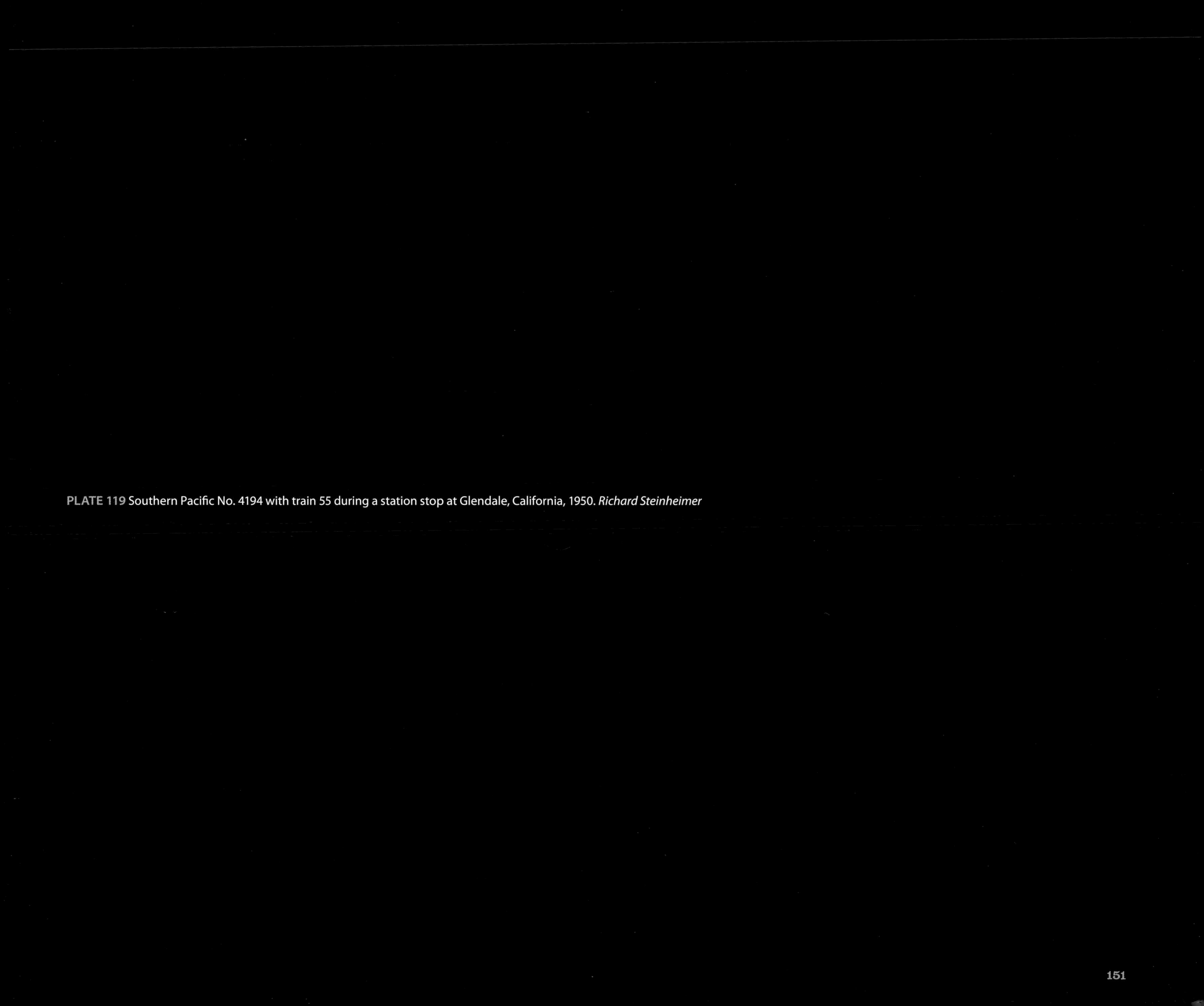

PLATE 119 Southern Pacific No. 4194 with train 55 during a station stop at Glendale, California, 1950. *Richard Steinheimer*

CANADIAN RAILWAYS HAVE ATTRACTED American railway photographers for generations. Both Canadian National and the Canadian Pacific have always been tidy, well-run lines, featuring excellent track, American-style operations, and tightly scheduled trains. They were also home to handsome steam power. While both railroads' engines were characterized by well-proportioned designs, each was famous for the distinctive appearance of its engines, and each favored different types of engines.

CN had assembled a large fleet of modern eight-coupled types, specifically 4-8-2 Mountains and 4-8-4 Northerns (or Confederations as they were more commonly known on CN). By American standards, CN's 4-8-4s were relative lightweights. The use of four sets of driving wheels allowed for a powerful engine with relatively low axle weight, which resulted in great route availability; 4-8-4s could be used in both freight and passenger service on most main lines, unlike some heavy American 4-8-4s that were restricted to specific routes because of their weight.

CP bought 2-8-2 Mikados, primarily for freight, and sampled the 4-8-4, buying just two, which spent most of their careers on the Montreal–Toronto sleeping-car run. For the most part, CP shunned the larger modern eight-coupled types.

Traditionally CP had favored six-coupled types. Early on it had standardized on the 4-6-0 Ten-Wheeler and later bought large numbers of 4-6-2 Pacifics. It was also among the largest users of the 4-6-4 Hudson, a type made famous by CP's *Royal Hudsons* (so named because two of

their class hauled specials carrying King George VI and Queen Elizabeth in 1939). CP's steam was unusually elegant. In the 1930s, the railroad applied conservative streamlining to many of its locomotives, including the *Royal Hudsons*. Even its largest engines, the 2-10-4 Selkirk types were semi-streamlined.

Canadian railways refrained from wide-scale dieselization longer than most roads in the United States. But while Canadian dieselization was implemented later, once it was underway it was accomplished swiftly; however, ardent American steam enthusiasts could still find mainline steam running north of the border when just about everyone stateside had gone diesel. CN steam finished in mid-1959; CP held out until early 1960.

As the end game approached in Canada, the task of finding steam was made simpler as engines were concentrated at primary eastern hubs. For the steam photographer, a trip to Canada was a must. For those who had just caught the tail end of steam operations in the United States, Canada offered a brief window to it.

Montreal was Canada's ground zero for steam. The intensity of operations here meant that a lot of steam was still working late in the game. For the casual enthusiast, summer might seem like an ideal time to visit, but for a photographer, winter offered greater drama, with condensation in subzero temperatures making for spectacular effluence as engines started out or rolled tonnage over icy rails.

For Ron Wright and his friends, an epic eleventh-hour trip to Quebec in December 1959 and January 1960 proved well-timed and exceptionally productive.

Careful planning, good luck, and persistence paid out handsomely; they were rewarded with many outstanding photographs in the final days of regular CP steam operation.

In December 1959, Ron was just sixteen years old and living in Rochester, New York. He traveled by New York Central to Albany where he was joined by Victor Hand, Don Phillips, and Willie Westcott, all eager young steam enthusiasts. From there, the group traveled to Montreal on the Delaware & Hudson.

"It was sad; steam was at its end. We knew the final day [for Canadian Pacific steam] was going to be soon, and it would probably end at Montreal," Ron recalled. "CN had already finished. But, I was very focused, and the longer we could get away to photograph steam the better. We had ten days around Christmas and New Year's."

At that time, while there was still plenty of steam on the move, diesels had arrived, along with Budd rail diesel cars. Finding working steam was a challenge. Ron remembered that Hand did a lot of the planning. "Victor was very good with the timetables, and using deduction he seemed to know which trains were likely to run," Ron says. "Other times we'd just go down to the roundhouse and ask the foreman which engines were going out that day." Ron explained that the men on the CP were friendly to them, but admits that they would take photos before seeking out the foreman. Just in case.

Christmas was an ideal time for steam. Ordinarily, a train might be scheduled as a Budd Rail Diesel Car (RDC), but because of the holidays CP was running long trains and extra trains that were more likely to warrant steam. While they worked intensely to catch as many engines as they could, Ron still remembered the one that got away.

"I heard the Scoot departing from the hotel," he says, referring to CP's local run from Montreal to St. John via Brownville Junction, Maine. "We watched it leave town, steam from the locomotive trailing behind it. Although we missed that train, we caught the westbound Scoot arriving later that day."

While fantastic for visual effect, the extreme cold was hard on the boys and their equipment. By that time, Ron had invested in a Rolleicord, a well-made German twin-lens reflex popular with railway photographers for its ease of use and excellent optics. "It was bitterly cold. So cold, that you didn't know if the camera was going to work," Ron recalls. "The shutter might freeze and you'd get nothing. While my Rolleicord did pretty good, some of the other guys didn't fair so well."

Missing photographic opportunities when they were so close at hand was a photographer's worst nightmare, especially when they might never have another chance to see steam on the CP. As it happened, steam ended a few weeks later, although it returned briefly in the spring of that year, before concluding for good.

"For us, January was pretty much the end," Ron says.

PLATE 120 Canadian National Railway No. 6258 waits to depart westbound at Brockville, Ontario, August 23, 1958. *Jim Shaughnessy*

PLATE 121 Canadian National
No. 6249 heads compass north near
Long Branch near Toronto, October
1953. *J. William Vigrass*

PLATE 123 Canadian Pacific No. 3101 leads the *Ocean Limited* westbound at Oxford Lake, west of Magog, Quebec, August 29, 1954. *Jim Shaughnessy*

PLATE 122 Canadian Pacific No. 29 at Chipman, New Brunswick,
August 9, 1956. *George C. Corey*

PLATE 124 Canadian Pacific Class G4 Pacific No. 2451 works alongside new Budd rail diesel cars (RDCs) at Montreal, December 26, 1959. *Ron Wright*

PLATE 125 Trailing view of Canadian Pacific No. 2451 (opposite) at Montreal, December 26, 1959. *Ron Wright*

PLATE 126 Head-on view of the smokebox door on Canadian Pacific No. 1083, Vallée Jonction, Quebec, New Year's Eve 1959. *Ron Wright*

PLATE 127 Crosshead on Canadian Pacific No. 5107 at Megantic, Quebec, January 1, 1960. *Ron Wright*

PLATE 128 Canadian National's passenger train from Montreal hits the Canadian Pacific diamonds at Lennoxville, Quebec, May 28, 1955.
Jim Shaughnessy

PLATE 129 Canadian National
2-10-2 No. 4102 works in freight
transfer service near Montreal,
November 25, 1955. *Jim Shaughnessy*

PLATE 130 Canadian Pacific 4-6-0 No. 1039 leads a Quebec Central freight south of Vallée Jonction, Quebec, May 29, 1959.
Jim Shaughnessy

PLATE 132 A Quebec Central snowplow extra works across a truss bridge at Vallée Jonction, Quebec, New Year's Eve 1959. *Ron Wright*

PLATE 131 Canadian Pacific No. 5147 hauls a Christmas-day
special at Westmount, Montreal, 1959. *Ron Wright*

PLATE 133 Quebec Central 1083 works across a grade crossing at Megantic, Quebec, January 1, 1960. *Ron Wright*

CAPTIONS

PLATE 1 (TITLE PAGE)

Among the railroads that resisted dieselization was U.S. Steel's Duluth, Missabe & Iron Range, a compact but heavily built railroad focused on moving iron ore from the Minnesota Iron Ranges to Lake Superior ports. After World War II, the Missabe looked to other U.S. Steel roads for surplus steam and acquired a modern fleet of 2-10-4s from the Bessemer & Lake Erie. Ultimately, the Missabe capitulated to diesels, but the process wasn't completed until 1960, several years after most other American roads. *John E. Pickett*

PLATE 2

Gainesville Midland had six locomotives to serve its 42-mile line that ran from a Southern Railway interchange at Gainesville to Athens, Georgia, where it connected with the Seaboard Air Line. *Gordon S. Crowell*

PLATE 3

During its transition from steam to diesel, Central Vermont often mixed motive power on its freights. In this view, a northward freight crosses the Millers Falls high bridge with one of CV's revered 2-8-0s in the lead. Behind it is a pair of Fairbanks-Morse C-Liner diesels borrowed from CV's parent, Canadian National. In the final years of steam operation, when steam and diesels were mixed, the diesels tended to lead. These diesels didn't serve for long on the CV, however. By the late 1950s, the railroad had dieselized with its own fleet of EMD GP9s and Alco switchers. *Jim Shaughnessy*

PLATE 4

New York Central's Boston & Albany was among the first major routes in the East to be completely dieselized. Owing to the line's steep grades, B&A's freight operations were largely dieselized by the late-1940s, while passenger steam survived a little longer. Officially, steam ended on Monday, April 16, 1951, when New York Central Mohawk No. 3004, specially polished for the occasion, brought train 33, The Wolverine (Boston via Canada to Chicago Central Station), west under swollen skies. Rain didn't dampen interest in the event. Both Robert Buck and Warren St. George rolled the train by to make photographs. *Robert A. Buck*

PLATE 5

In later years, it was common to find New York Central's 4-8-2 Mohawks working some through Boston & Albany passenger trains. By 1950, steam was nearing its end on the B&A, as parent New York Central was quick to dieselize the graded route. Today, Riverside is unrecognizable from this scene. The railroad has been reduced to two tracks; it runs near the multilane Massachusetts Turnpike and crosses the even wider I-95/Route 128. *George C. Corey*

PLATE 6

In 1900, the New York Central & Hudson River leased the Boston & Albany, leading to the predominance of the New York Central System image on the B&A for a few years. Local protests restored the B&A name, and from 1912 through the end of the steam era, most equipment, including locomotives like this A1b 2-8-4 Berkshire, was lettered for the line. *Robert A. Buck*

PLATE 7

In the 1940s, Robert Buck rode and photographed both steam- and diesel-powered trains on the length of New York Central's Boston & Albany line. His fascination with his hometown railroad allowed him to produce a valuable record of its final years of steam operations, including this image made in the especially harsh winter of 1947. *Robert A. Buck*

PLATE 8

The southward Boston section of the Green Mountain Flyer departed Rutland, Vermont, in the early afternoon and immediately began climbing toward the summit near Mt. Holly. Leading this day is Rutland's Pacific type No. 85. Built by Alco in 1929, this locomotive was retired in early 1953. Although Rutland remained loyal to steam until after World War II, the railroad dieselized rapidly between 1950 and 1952, replacing all of its steam with new Alco road-switchers and a lone General Electric switcher. *John E. Pickett*

PLATE 9

Among John Pickett's favorite railroads was the Vermont-based Rutland. In the period of a few years he made between fifteen and twenty trips to photograph the line and even wrote a college thesis about the railroad. This view was exposed on 616 film and shows the Green Mountain Flyer departing Rutland, Vermont, for the south. *John E. Pickett*

PLATE 10

Among Boston & Maine's last steam engines were the venerable 2-6-0 Moguls assigned to Boston-area suburban services, such as engine No. 1493 photographed in 1955 on the Central Mass line. *George C. Corey*

PLATES 11 AND 12

Central Vermont's Stateline Hill south of Palmer, Massachusetts, was a popular place to catch steam at work. Shortly after the line left Palmer Yard it crossed the Quaboag River and began its steady climb through the town of Monson. While less than 1.3 percent, this prolonged grade proved a trial for CV's 2-8-0s like these, which had ruled the line for four decades. The railroad crossed the parallel highway Route 32 at several locations, and Robert Buck often waited for trains at the grade crossing in South Monson and then raced to either Smith's Bridge at Stafford Hollow Road or the Route 32 crossing at the summit, just shy of the Connecticut state line. Having witnessed the most dramatic part of the run, Robert could then return toward Palmer for action on the Boston & Albany or head home to nearby Warren. *Both Robert A. Buck*

PLATE 13

Toward the end of a run to New London, Connecticut, Robert Buck made this trailing view from the cab of Central Vermont 2-8-0 as it worked south along the Thames River south of Norwich, Connecticut, on January 9, 1955. *Robert A. Buck*

PLATE 14

Robert Buck had the fireman's view from a Central Vermont 2-8-0 as it worked southbound through Monson, Massachusetts, on its way to the summit at Stateline on January 9, 1955. He had written ahead for permission to ride the line and was granted a final trip from Palmer, Massachusetts, to New London, Connecticut. Getting back home again proved a challenge since CV no longer operated a scheduled passenger service. *Robert A. Buck*

PLATE 15

In 1955, Onawa Bridge was a difficult and isolated location to reach. Jim Shaughnessy knew Canadian Pacific dispatcher Jim Britt at Brownville, Maine, and organized for him and a friend to ride out to the bridge on the westbound "Scoot," CPR's local run between Montreal and St. John via Brownville Junction. This train is the eastbound Scoot, which was both the subject of the photo and their ride back to Brownville. Britt had wired instructions to the train to collect the pair of photographers at Onawa. Otherwise, it would have been a long walk home. *Jim Shaughnessy*

PLATE 16

Pennsy's K4s Pacifics were among the most celebrated American passenger locomotives. Characterized by a big boiler with high drivers and a well-balanced appearance, the K4s ("s" for superheated) led Pennsy's passenger trains for four decades. By the mid-1950s, diesels had taken over most of the premier runs (outside of electrified territory), leaving only short runs like this one between Philadelphia and Atlantic City for Pennsy's remaining Pacifics. This view of Pennsy's five-track electrified line was exposed from Girard Avenue in Philadelphia. Steam under wire wasn't unusual for trains that continued on nonelectrified lines. Pennsy and Reading shared the Atlantic City run and at the time of this image both railroads were still assigning steam locomotives to these trains. *John E. Pickett*

PLATE 17

This I1-class 2-10-0 Decapod was one of the last locomotives Ron Wright shot on his April 1957 visit to East Altoona. "I took this picture off the bridge near the roundhouse," he recalls. "Our time was up, and we were waiting for one of our group to finish. I wish I'd made a view looking the other direction toward the roundhouse. That would have been my pride and joy. I don't know why I didn't." *Ron Wright*

PLATE 18

New York Central was a busy line with a continuous parade of steam locomotives, including the railroad's famous 4-6-4 Hudsons, 4-8-4 Niagaras, and 4-8-2 Mohawks, such as engine 2748, pictured here with a long freight. In the mid-1940s, John Pickett was enthralled with trains but gave little thought to dieselization, which would replace steam in just a few years. "Diesels were just a distant threat," he recalls. *John E. Pickett*

PLATE 19

This new G-3 Pacific is leading a passenger train bound for Philadelphia. "When we photographed that Pacific it was just a year and half old," John Pickett recalls. Pickett also remembered that there were tricks to photographing the Reading and that it helped to be accompanied by local photographers. "You had to be careful around the Reading," he says, "they weren't friendly to railfans, not like some railroads. Gordon, Pennsylvania, was tricky, and you had to be especially careful there." *John E. Pickett*

PLATE 20

John Pickett made this image of a Reading 2-10-2 on one of his forays into the anthracite fields of northeastern Pennsylvania with Fred Kern and Bert Pennypacker. The trio had been following this slow-moving freight in Fred's Chevy sedan. "Fred would always drive us," John recalls. "He was a bit older, a nice guy but kind of gruff. At this spot there was a tunnel right behind us. That night we stayed in a guesthouse. It was only three dollars, but I didn't have much money then." Although the anthracite railroads were in a sharp decline by 1950, there was still plenty of action to find. Reading Company held off dieselization longer than many of its neighbors. *John E. Pickett*

PLATE 21

Baltimore & Ohio acquired Buffalo & Susquehanna in the 1930s as part of an expansionist scheme that didn't fully pan out. After a flood washed out a portion of the B&S in 1942, the railroad's former lines were an isolated system disconnected from the rest of the B&O network, contributing to technological stagnation. As a result, operations on the B&S were a throwback to an earlier time. By the late 1940s, its early-twentieth-century 2-8-0s were reminiscent of operations forty years earlier. Gordon Roth made this image while studying photography at the Rochester Institute of Technology. He and his roommate Bob Perko drove down from Rochester in a 1930 Ford Model A and camped out overnight to wait for the train. *Gordon R. Roth*

PLATE 22

Baltimore & Ohio's EM-1s were the last 2-8-8-4 Yellowstones built by Baldwin. Delivered during World War II, the EM-1 was a compromise between the War Production Board and B&O: the railroad desperately needed more freight power and had hoped to order EMD FT diesels, but settled for modern Baldwin steam when the board denied its request. John Pickett recalls that the EM-1s, "were exceptionally handsome engines, well-proportioned, and good to look at. It's a pity B&O didn't save one." *John E. Pickett*

PLATE 23

West of Meyersdale on its ascent of Sand Patch, the Baltimore & Ohio followed a sweeping curve beneath Western Maryland's magnificent Connellsville Extension. That's where John Pickett made a stunning set of photographs of the eastward freight that he had been following for hours. Although Western Maryland's line was abandoned in the 1970s, the trestle survives as a rail trail. *John E. Pickett*

PLATE 24

At the time of this photograph west of Meyersdale, Baltimore & Ohio's S-1a-class 2-10-2 No. 6201 was nearing its thirtieth year of service. By contrast, the EM-1 leading the train worked for less than fifteen years before it was sidelined by diesels. *John E. Pickett*

PLATES 25 AND 26

Delaware & Hudson freight ran via Erie Railroad's line south of Lanesboro, Pennsylvania, over Ararat Summit toward Carbondale and Scranton. Prior to making these photographs, Gordon Roth had a conversation with the pusher crew at Cascade Wye and made arrangements with the engineer to provide lots of smoke from the Challenger on the climb toward Ararat. He exposed this sequence using a 5x7 Speed Graphic. The larger film size offered greater detail and tonality than the more common 4x5-inch film.

After World War II, the D&H was incredibly busy with coal traffic and sometimes required three 2-8-0 Consolidations on heavy trains. This boom faded quickly as a result of the switch from coal to oil for domestic home heating. Simultaneous with D&H's declining traffic was its own decision to switch from coal to oil in the form of new Alco diesels that rapidly displaced its 4-6-6-4 Challengers and other steam. *Both Gordon R. Roth*

PLATE 27

This view at Thompson is just a few miles south of Lanesboro, Pennsylvania, where Delaware & Hudson's line passed under Erie's main line at Starrucca Viaduct and connected with Erie's line south toward Scranton. Gordon Roth exposed this view of a D&H Challenger type while on his way to Rochester to take a Rochester Institute of Technology entrance exam. Gordon always tried to pick picturesque locations with some balance of trees and other scenic elements. *Gordon R. Roth*

PLATE 28

Although the locomotive is obscured by its own steam and smoke, this trailing steam-hauled view of Erie Stillwell suburban cars captures the spirit of steam power at work. Richard Young had a rare ability to make the ordinary appear fascinating. Scenes like this one were still common when he exposed the photo in February 1947, yet he succeeded in preserving a moment for posterity, perhaps recognizing that the commonplace would someday appear precious. *Richard H. Young, Solomon collection*

PLATE 29

Richard Young was an employee of the Erie Railroad and a prolific photographer. While many of his Erie photographs were exposed near the railroad's eastern terminus at Jersey City, Young traveled across the railroad making images that captured the essence of company operations and motive power. This image of one of Erie's Class S-4 2-8-4 Berkshires is a rare photograph, not only for Young's sophisticated use of light to maximize the drama (unusual in the steam era), but also because of the location. Relatively few steam action photographs were made along the Erie in far western New York. Young kept meticulous notes about his negatives. This photo was exposed at f4.5 at 1/100 second using Kodak Super XX. Erie had 105 Berkshires, all built from 1927 to 1929 by all three major builders. No. 3393 was among the last, a Lima machine built in 1929. *Richard H. Young, Solomon collection*

PLATES 30 AND 31

Although Pennsylvania Railroad steam was nearing its end when Ron Wright and his friends visited East Altoona on this clear, bright spring day in 1957, there were still plenty of engines under steam. These photographs were made on a trip called "The 1957 Motorcade" organized by Jack Collins, John Prophet, and other members of the Rochester & Buffalo Enthusiasts. "There were five or six cars [of photographers]," Ron recalls. "The Rochester guys met those coming down from Buffalo at Salamanca, New York. We were looking for Pennsy steam wherever we could find it. We visited Renovo and Lock Haven, Pennsylvania, and followed an M1 [4-8-2 Mountain type] down the Bald Eagle Branch to Tyrone. The roundhouse foreman at East Altoona was something of a railfan and he gave us the run of the place for an hour. I had cinders in my shoes at the end of the hour and it hurt to walk."

Ron adds, "The coal dock there was built the month I was born: November 1943." As a teenager, he knew he was witnessing the end of an era. A few months later, PRR had dumped the fires for good. *Both Ron Wright*

PLATES 32 AND 33

Pennsy's four-track Middle Division (Harrisburg to Altoona) was a favorite for photographers because of its accessibility, splendid scenery, and continuous parade of freight and passenger trains. Pennsy's big-boiler M1 Mountain types like those seen here were standard mainline freight power from the mid-1920s until the diesels took over. The M1 shared the boiler used by the I1s 2-10-0 "Hippo." Where the I1s was intended for slow-speed drag freight work, the M1 was designed for relatively fast mainline running. These were good-looking locomotives and made for great photos. *Both John E. Pickett*

PLATE 34

"I was traveling with Bruce Black," John Pickett begins. "We had slept in the car south of Northumberland and then drove to the yard where we found this ore train. We followed it up the line from Northumberland toward Delano. This traffic was interchanged with Lehigh Valley. Bruce was on his way to Chicago. After we were done making pictures, I dropped him along Route 20 at Sharon Springs, New York. The New York State Thruway had just opened and Bruce had to wait a long time for a ride."

This episode illustrates the dramatic changes in American transportation in the mid-1950s. Not only was the steam locomotive in its death throes, but intercity railroad traffic was being siphoned to roadways as a result of the massive federal highway program. The situation was especially acute in the eastern states, where multiple-track mainlines reached across the region. As traditional traffic was drained from railroads, new businesses tended to locate near highways. *John E. Pickett*

PLATES 35 THROUGH 41

Pennsylvania Railroad's Elmira Branch was a single-track line extending from north-central Pennsylvania via Elmira, New York, to a Lake Ontario coal pier at Sodus Point, New York. In the 1920s, the Pennsy had expanded the pier, which measured 885 feet long and 58 feet high, and contained eight coal pockets designed to simultaneously feed two lake boats. Traffic moving via the branch came from myriad places. Coal trains came off the Main Line via Tyrone traveling northeastward on the Bald Eagle Branch to Lock Haven, then on to Williamsport, Pennsylvania. Some traffic flowed via Keating, Renovo, and Lock Haven, or traveled northward on the Northern Central via Sunbury and Northumberland. Coal was classified at Pennsy's Southport, New York, yards near Elmira.

During the mid-1950s the Elmira Branch was exceptionally busy and Jim Shaughnessy took good advantage of this late steam-era traffic swell that helped keep the railroad's I1s, L1s, and M1s in steam for a few more years. Operations often required helpers (in some situations, diesels), creating some excellent opportunities for transitional photos. Yet the boom was temporary. Steam was gone by 1957. Within another decade the coal traffic faded from the line and Sodus Point was closed as result of competition from the St. Lawrence Seaway. *All Jim Shaughnessy*

PLATE 44

Ron Wright would take the New York Central to Buffalo. "From Central Terminal, I'd walk to Nickel Plate's yard at South Park, instead of taking the bus," he says. "That way I'd save twenty five cents. As a kid, I'd think nothing about walking." In this view, the Alco switcher behind the 0-8-0 is a telling sign of what was to come. *Ron Wright*

PLATE 45

In this atmospheric view made on a gray October day, two Nickel Plate Road locomotives simmer among yards full of boxcars that were still the standard rail freight vehicle. But Nickel Plate was an intermodal pioneer and one of the only roads to move piggyback behind steam. A couple of early intermodal "trailer on flat car" shipments are visible at left. *Ron Wright*

PLATE 42

East Broad Top was among America's last surviving narrow-gauge common carriers. This 33-mile line primarily brought product from central Pennsylvania coal mines to a connection with the Pennsylvania Railroad at Mount Union. By the 1950s the railroad's three-foot-gauge track and early-twentieth-century shops at Rockhill Furnace made it among the most antique railroads in the East. Although the EBT shut down as a common carrier in 1956, a short portion of the line and some of its Baldwin 2-8-2 Mikados were revived as a tourist attraction in 1960. They entertained generations of visitors until excursion service was suspended in 2011. *Gordon S. Crowell*

PLATE 43

Nickel Plate's Berkshires were one of the finest examples of the 2-8-4 arrangement developed by Lima Locomotive Works in the mid-1920s as an expansion of the 2-8-2 Mikado. Significantly, Nickel Plate No. 779 was the last new steam locomotive built by Lima. It was only eight years old at the time of Jim Shaughnessy's iconic photograph, and by the end of the following year it would be cold. The locomotive was preserved and today is displayed near where it was built at Lima, Ohio. *Jim Shaughnessy*

PLATE 46

Nickel Plate Road was the last big steam show in western New York State. It continued to work road freights with its 2-8-4 Berkshires for several years after other railroads had dieselized their mainline operations in Buffalo. *Ron Wright*

PLATE 47

Ron Wright photographed Nickel Plate's fast freight, called the "Flying Saucer," from Ridge Road in Lackawanna (a Buffalo suburb). Though he had walked there all the way from Buffalo Central Station, it was going to be a long a walk back, and he realized he might not make it in time to catch his train back home to Rochester. "I put my thumb out and hitched a ride on a [Buffalo Creek] diesel back to Nickel Plate's yard at South Park [near Central Station]," he recalls. He made a few more steam photos in the process, like this one, which he might not have otherwise.

The Buffalo Creek Railroad was a short line jointly leased by the Lehigh Valley and Erie Railroad that provided terminal switching in the Buffalo area. *Ron Wright*

PLATE 48

"At Rochester, I'd catch either New York Central's train 35 [The Iroquois] or train 59 [The Chicagoan]," Ron Wright recalls. "I'd always sit on the south side of the train. West of Buffalo my eyes were glued to the tracks. Nickel Plate ran its freights at forty to fifty miles per hour, while Central's passenger trains would travel at seventy to eighty miles per hour." In this instance, Ron's train is overtaking a Nickel Plate freight (a common enough event) led by the last of the road's Lima-built 2-8-4s. The two lines were adjacent much of the way from Buffalo to Cleveland.

In 1957, New York Central started to thin its passenger schedule and only one morning train stopped in Rochester, which limited Ron's time on the Nickel Plate. On November 23, 1957, his destination was Dunkirk, New York. *Ron Wright*

PLATE 49

Dunkirk was one of Ron Wright's favorite places to photograph the Nickel Plate. The tower made for a warm refuge and allowed insight on operations because the operators knew when trains got close, controlling switches and signals while copying and handing train orders to dispatchers. This wintry silhouette at Dunkirk captures the feeling of steam working through backyards in the semi-industrial landscape of western New York. *Ron Wright.*

PLATE 50

Not all great photos are made on clear, sunny days. Bill Vigrass made the most of a foggy winter day while traveling with Nickel Plate Road company photographer Willis McCaleb to capture this Hudson working in passenger service between Rocky River and Lorain. By this date, Nickel Plate's regular passenger trains were hauled by Alco PA diesels and steam worked only special passenger trains. Pictured here is The Cinerama Special, carrying a trainload of film fans to Cleveland to view a traveling Cinerama show. Bill's brand-new 1956 Ford can be seen at the side of the road on the far right edge of the photo.

No. 170 was one of Nickel Plate's Alco built 4-6-4 Hudsons. These were delivered in 1927, shortly after New York Central's famous Hudsons. Despite Nickel Plate's pioneering application of the 4-6-4, these locomotives seem obscure compared to the Central's large fleet. *J. William Vigrass*

PLATE 51

Although the Nickel Plate was officially the New York, Chicago & St Louis, almost everyone referred to it by its trade name. Nine years after this image was made, Nickel Plate was blended into the expanding Norfolk & Western network. The near tracks are those of Cleveland Union Terminal, which had recently converted from electric to diesel operations and was taking the wires down. Nickel Plate Road was headquartered in Cleveland. *J. William Vigrass*

PLATE 52

Railway enthusiasts loved to cheer the underdog. In the mid-1950s, Nickel Plate's continued use of steam on its largely single-track main line running parallel to New York Central's four-track Water Level Route made photographers smile. *Jim Shaughnessy*

PLATE 53

In 1957, Jim Shaughnessy made trips to visit fellow photographer Craig Woodworth in Buffalo. "I'd travel west from Albany on a Friday afternoon on New York Central's *Ohio State*, and we'd head out on Saturday morning," he says. "At that stage, New York Central was dieselized. On this trip we focused on the Nickel Plate. Time was always a factor and you had to turn your back on some things because there was so much going on. . . . That's Craig posing as a railroad worker." The drive wheels on the shop floor are for the out-of-service 2-8-4 in the background. *Jim Shaughnessy*

PLATE 54

Nickel Plate, which didn't complete mainline dieselization until 1958, had continued to order new steam as late as 1949, including this Lima-built 2-8-4 delivered in May of that year. While some New York Central steam lingered into the mid-1950s, most of its mainline operations between Buffalo and Cleveland were diesel-powered by the early 1950s. *Jim Shaughnessy*

PLATE 55

For John Pickett the main attraction of Norfolk & Western was its busy east-west main line in the mountains of Virginia on both sides of Roanoke; however, on this drive from Philadelphia he followed Norfolk & Western's single-track Shenandoah Valley line to Roanoke, which relieved the tedium of the long drive and made for occasional photographic opportunities. *John E. Pickett*

PLATES 56 AND 57

The 2-6-6-4s were the Cadillac of Norfolk & Western's steam fleet. Powerful and fast, they worked time freights in mainline service, showering the line in steam and cinders. "Those were my favorite," John Pickett says. "I really liked the N&W A's." *Both John E. Pickett*

PLATE 58

This freight wasn't far behind Norfolk & Western's *Powhatan Arrow*. "On the mainline, those Y class could really move along," John Pickett explains. "They weren't slow engines." N&W's big Y class were the ultimate example of the compound steam locomotive in America. Compounds had been widely used in the late nineteenth and early twentieth centuries as a means of saving fuel and water through double expansion of the steam. The mallet-articulated compound was a variation introduced to North American operation by the Baltimore & Ohio in 1904; ultimately, hundreds of mallets were built for lines all around the country. *John E. Pickett*

PLATE 59

John Pickett was thrilled to catch some of Norfolk & Western's streamlined K-class 4-8-2 Mountain types. As he explains, "These were older engines from the 1920s that the railroad had overhauled and streamlined to look like the Js." The *Powhatan Arrow* was among N&W's streamlined named trains that connected Norfolk and Cincinnati. It was also a day train; its counterpart was an overnight service named *The Pocahontas* after the Native American princess. *John E. Pickett*

PLATE 60

During the 1930s Norfolk & Western refined the simple articulated for fast mainline service. It was one of only a few railroads to adopt the 2-6-6-4 wheel arrangement and had more of the type than any other line. These were its famous A class, featuring 70-inch drivers. At 35 to 40 miles per hour an A-class could develop roughly 5,500 horsepower. Although largely a freight locomotive in later years, an A-class could easily run at 70 miles per hour with a passenger train. *John E. Pickett*

PLATE 61

The sight of two Norfolk & Western Y-class Mallets with a mile of coal hoppers in tow was one of the great experiences of the steam era. *John E. Pickett*

PLATES 62 AND 63

In 1956, not only was Norfolk & Western still largely steam-powered, but the railroad was extremely busy. "I never waited very long for a train," John Pickett recalls. In just a few days it was possible to make a lot of railroad action photographs. In the 1980s, Norfolk Southern restored N&W No. 1218 to service as a star excursion engine. Yet photographs of 1218 in regular revenue service are relatively rare. *Both John E. Pickett*

PLATE 64

Norfolk & Western's streamlined J-class 4-8-4 is an American classic. A product of the railroad's Roanoke Shops, it was known for its great looks and exceptional performance. Norfolk & Western's mainline was equipped with Centralized Traffic Control that allowed dispatchers to run trains on either track in both directions on signal indication. *John E. Pickett*

PLATE 65

Norfolk & Western's final J-class 4-8-4 was the last new passenger steam locomotive built in the United States. When John Pickett exposed this photo, No. 613 was a still new machine, built in 1950, a year after Electro-Motive Division introduced its improved E8 passenger diesel model. Sadly, like many late-era steam locomotives, No. 613 had a short career. For railroads like the Norfolk & Western, the economics of steam operation changed quickly in the early 1950s. It went from building its own new steam locomotives to complete dieselization in just seven years. *John E. Pickett*

PLATE 66

Norfolk & Western's J-class 4-8-4s were its last and finest passenger steam, reaching speeds of 110 miles per hour in test runs. They were smooth-running engines much loved by crews and photographers, alike. The most famous J is No. 611, which was preserved after being retired from regular service in 1959. Restored to service in 1982, it toured the Norfolk Southern system for a dozen years, making it one of the most photographed engines in America. Today it is displayed at the Virginia Museum of Transportation in Roanoke, on a site near the location of this 1956 photograph of its less famous sister. *John E. Pickett*

PLATE 67

"The Alleghenies had been in and out of storage," Phil Weibler recalls. "Our engineer had been working branches and showed up for the run in shirtsleeves thinking he was getting a nice set of new diesels. He had a tough time with the Allegheny. It was an elephant on ice skates. He kept slipping the drivers. His fireman gave him instructions. Finally, to get started he ran ahead with the engine alone with sanders on and rail washers off."

Chesapeake & Ohio had a different train-operating philosophy than Norfolk & Western. Where N&W had figured out how to amply power a train to get it over the mountain quickly, C&O would load a locomotive to its practical limits and then struggle along at 2 miles per hour. *Philip A. Weibler*

PLATE 68

Chesapeake & Ohio's 2-6-6-6 Allegheny type is now credited as the heaviest locomotive to work American rails. First built in 1942, the 2-6-6-6 is believed to be slightly heavier than the Union Pacific's Big Boys. Lima built sixty 2-6-6-6s for C&O and another eight for the Virginian. While historians may argue over technical specifications, for the photographer, capturing a C&O Allegheny at work was a great thrill. *Philip A. Weibler*

PLATE 69

Chesapeake & Ohio was a coal-conveyor belt. Massive trains like this rolled over the main line taking mine products eastward to Newport News where C&O operated immense port facilities on the north side of the Hampton Roads estuary opposite Norfolk. Because of its affinity for coal, C&O delayed dieselization longer than many railroads, but by 1956, when Phil Weibler made this image, steam had almost faded from the scene and diesels worked most trains. *Philip A. Weibler*

PLATE 70

For many people growing up in the motor age, the railway was experienced through the window of the family car—perhaps a roadside glimpse of a train roaring along or brief glance of a wisp of steam across a field. In Jim Shaughnessy's case, he used the car as a tool for photography, both to chase the train and, in this instance, to frame it in the car window. "I was with Sandy 'SS' Worthen from Montreal," Jim recalls. "We were chasing this Baltimore & Ohio branch line local that gathered coal cars from regional mines." *Jim Shaughnessy*

PLATE 71

The Emory River Railroad was a 13-mile-long line that ran from coal mines at Mahan, Tennessee, to an interchange with the Southern Railway at Lancing. Gordon Crowell made a pilgrimage in 1953 to capture its only locomotive on film, thus preserving it for posterity. *Gordon S. Crowell*

PLATE 72

Louisville & Nashville's line laced through eastern Kentucky coal country, serving myriad mines and load-outs. No. 1895 was a Baldwin-built 2-8-2 Mikado, a type that commonly worked L&N freights until dieselization was completed in the mid-1950s. Notice the engine number printed in the headlight. This was a practice peculiar to that railroad in the steam era. *Gordon S. Crowell*

PLATE 73

Views like this show the great variety of equipment on the move during the steam-to-diesel transition. Gallery cars and steam coexisted for a very short time. The Pacific had been a staple of North Western passenger service for more than forty years, but the gallery-style bi-levels were brand-new (some would serve for another four to five decades as they remained the standard type for Chicago-area suburban services). The new Electro-Motive F-Units to the right are on a long-distance train. *Philip A. Weibler*

PLATE 74

When the photographer and his family first moved to Quincy in 1952, they lived in a house near this location. The sounds of trains climbing the grade have stayed with him for sixty years; however, he notes that "by the time I took this photograph, we'd moved across town." The engine pictured is an elderly O1a class 2-8-2. Behind it is a canteen style tender. Regular steam out of Quincy concluded at the end of 1953, a few days after this image was exposed. *Philip A. Weibler*

PLATE 75

Illinois Central was a railroad that not only built many of its own locomotives but also kept steam working longer than many of its neighboring lines. Big steam worked IC coal country through the 1950s, although seasonal traffic fluctuations sometimes found engines stored for weeks or even months between work. On Labor Day weekend 1957, Jim Shaughnessy, Ray Buhrmaster, and John Pickett made a productive visit to IC's hub at Paducah, Kentucky, where they found a lot of steam still at work. *Jim Shaughnessy*

PLATE 76

The photographer describes this dynamic image as "my accidental pan shot." Unlike planned panned photos, when the photographer deliberately selects a slower shutter speed and swings the camera in the direction of train travel, in this instance when Phil Weibler released the shutter on his Baby Brownie Special, he unintentionally pushed too hard, forcing the camera laterally. Regardless of how it was accomplished, the photograph is a winner and captures this 4-6-0 type for posterity. *Philip A. Weibler*

PLATE 77

By the early 1950s, 4-4-2 Atlantics were rare birds. In fact, No. 395 is on a fan trip that will be the class's last run. All the while, an Electro-Motive GP7 road switcher lurks in the distance. In the early twentieth century, the Atlantic type had been a popular wheel arrangement for express passenger service. C&NW's D Class were products of Alco's Schenectady, New York, shops and built between 1900 and 1908. The advent of heavier steel coaches and longer trains found the 4-4-2 type underpowered for many runs. As a result, larger types, such as the 4-6-2 Pacific, found favor. Most of C&NWs Atlantics had been scrapped by World War II, so in the early 1950s survivors of the type were relics, which made a photo of an Atlantic in service especially rare. *Philip A. Weibler*

PLATE 78

Chicago & North Western's Chicago terminal was completed in June 1911, some forty-four years before this photo was exposed. This was more than just the railroad's Chicago passenger station; it was by far the busiest and most important passenger facility on the whole railroad. *Philip A. Weibler*

PLATE 79

Among the engines under steam on this atmospheric morning were Chicago & North Western Atlantic No. 395 (one of two assigned to West Chicago in the early 1950s), a Pacific type, and one of the railroad's omnipresent R-1 Ten-Wheelers. Philip A. Weibler recalled that the same engines had worked the same trains on the C&NW from the 1930s to the 1950s, often assigned to the same terminals for years at a time. While the engines remained the same, the tenders were changed because they tended to rot out as a result of acid created when coal mixed with water. *Bob Meiborg photo, Philip A. Weibler collection*

PLATE 80

North Western's thirty-five big Class H 4-8-4s were built by Baldwin in 1929 and 1930 and intended for both heavy freight and passenger work. In their early years they worked only the railroad's West Line (Chicago to Omaha); after World War II their territory was expanded. The class was upgraded from H to class H-1, which included modern equipment such as lightweight Boxpok disc drivers (as pictured). It was typical for a 4-8-4 to work out to Omaha on a freight and come back with a passenger train. No. 3031 often worked train 13, the *Omaha Express*, which carried as many as twenty cars of mail and express and a coach—and needed a big engine to haul it. *Philip A. Weibler*

PLATE 81

No. 5634 was one of ten O-5As built by Burlington's West Burlington Shops in 1940. These were the last of the class, which totaled twenty-eight locomotives (plus eight of the older Class O 4-8-4s built by Baldwin). John E. Pickett and Jim Shaughnessy made a memorable trip together to catch the final months of Burlington steam. *John E. Pickett*

PLATE 82

Located on the eastern bank of the Mississippi, 262 miles from Chicago, Quincy was an important hub on the Burlington (and the "Q" in the road's official name: Chicago, Burlington & Quincy). The Burlington remained a hotbed of big steam operations into the mid-1950s, a few years longer than other railroads in the region. *Philip A. Weibler*

PLATE 83

Burlington's 2-10-4s were extremely powerful engines built by Baldwin in the late 1920s, and later rebuilt at the company shops. They were typically assigned to Illinois coal trains like this one. Burlington operated a dense network that included main lines radiating out from Chicago, as well as various secondary connecting routes. Abingdon is on the line south of Galesburg running via Beardstown to southern Illinois. *Philip A. Weibler*

PLATE 84

The Wabash was the minority player at Quincy, where the big show in town was the Burlington. In this 1952 view, 0-6-0 No. 546 switches a beer distributor in town. The photographer's use of panning captures the locomotive in motion, although it has the effect of making the locomotive seem like it was moving much faster than the ambling gait necessary on industrial trackage. Those workers clinging to the pilot weren't in nearly as much danger as they appear. Wabash was not often photographed, and its switch engines wouldn't have attracted the attention of many photographers, yet this scene captures a classic daily event as it would have occurred for decades. *Philip A. Weibler*

PLATE 85

Weight restrictions on the Wabash branch to Keokuk, Iowa, resulted in the use of steam on road freights until 1955, several years after most other Wabash services had been dieselized. In this view, one of Burlington's new Electro-Motive road switchers, GP7 No. 242, offers a vision of the future. Ultimately, Wabash gave up on its sixty-year-old 2-6-0 Moguls in favor of new road switchers. Today the colorfully painted GP7 would be popular with enthusiast photographers. *Philip A. Weibler*

PLATE 86

Steam locomotives were labor-intensive machines compared with diesels. In addition to regular fuel and water stops, ashes had to be dumped from the firebox, reciprocating parts required lubrication and inspection, and boilers need to be flushed, among numerous other small tasks. The introduction of diesels not only lowered labor and fuel costs but increased locomotive availability. By the mid-1950s, every railroad in America had accepted the advantages of the new technology. Scenes like this one, once common everywhere, vanished as diesels took over. *Philip A. Weibler*

PLATE 87

Bevier & Southern was an obscure 15.5-mile Missouri short line that fed coal traffic to the Burlington at its namesake. While the railroad kept its own locomotives in exceptionally good order, as this immaculately maintained example illustrates, it didn't treat borrowed Burlington steam with the same tender loving care. Interestingly, B&S was an early user of train radios. *Philip A. Weibler*

PLATE 88

Among the Midwest's short lines was Minnesota's Duluth & Northeastern, which operated slightly more than eleven miles of line between a connection with Duluth, Missabe & Iron Range at Saginaw and junctions with the Great Northern, Northern Pacific, and Milwaukee Road at Cloquet. Through the late 1950s, this railroad retained all the charm of a classic American branch line. In this view, the Union Pacific boxcar advertising "The Route of the Streamliners" nearly spoils the aura of the line with a 2-8-0 Consolidation that harked back to the pre–World War I era. Unlike so many locomotives that met a date with the blowtorch, No. 28 survived and is on display at Cloquet. *John E. Pickett*

PLATE 89

John Pickett counts Northern Pacific among his favorite roads from the steam era. In June 1953 he went on a fifteen-day railroad photography adventure before entering the U.S. Army. The scene was changing rapidly, but there was still a lot of steam working main lines; you just needed to get out there and catch it. "We were driving along and saw smoke and caught up with this train," John recalls. "We paced the engine for miles. It was carrying white flags, which told us it was an extra." Incidentally, NP was the first railroad to adopt the 4-8-4 type, whose "Northern" moniker was a nod to the railroad. No. 2676 is one of the A-4 class built by Baldwin in 1941. It was just twelve years old and near the end of its active life. *John E. Pickett*

PLATE 90

John E. Pickett was fortunate to experience Yellowstone types on both the Northern Pacific and the Missabe (not to mention Baltimore & Ohio's Class EM-1s). Northern Pacific was first to use the 2-8-8-4 wheel arrangement (type was named for its Yellowstone Division in eastern Montana and North Dakota). While NP's engines ended service in the mid-1950s and were all scrapped, the Missabe continued to operate its big engines until 1960, making them some of last big freight steam on the move in the United States. This engine is now displayed at the Lake Superior Transportation Museum in Duluth. *John E. Pickett*

PLATE 91

Rio Grande's Monarch Branch was unusually steep, even for the narrow-gauge system. Its grades exceeded four percent (a climb of four feet for every hundred traveled) and the line featured switchbacks to reach higher elevations, where a conventional line would have been impractically steep. *John E. Pickett*

PLATES 92 AND 93

In 1956, Rio Grande converted its three-foot-gauge Monarch Branch (running approximately twenty-one miles from Salida to Monarch, Colorado, via a portion of the old Marshall Pass route to Poncha Junction) to standard gauge and operated the line in its final years with diesels. This left the San Juan extension as its only narrow-gauge operation, which survived in steam until its abandonment. While portions of the San Juan extension survive as the Cumbres & Toltec and Durango & Silverton tourist roads, the Monarch Branch was finally abandoned in the early 1980s. *Philip A. Weibler (top) and Jim Shaughnessy (bottom)*

PLATE 94

Rio Grande's K-37-class 2-8-2 Mikados were originally standard-gauge 2-8-0s. They were rebuilt and regauged at the company's Burnham Shops from 1928 to 1930 and were its most powerful narrow-gauge steam locomotives. John Gruber's use of the pan effect (setting the camera to a relative slow shutter speed and moving with the subject parallel to the film plane) made this engine appear to be traveling much faster than it really was. *John Gruber*

PLATES 95 AND 96

John Gruber's pioneering use of 35mm Nikon cameras with long telephoto lenses for railway subjects distinguished his work from that of most other steam photographers. Although some of his steam images are now more than fifty years old, they have a modern look and remain among the most unusual in this book. *Both John Gruber*

PLATE 97

Denver & Rio Grande Western's three-foot-gauge operations in Colorado and New Mexico survived into the 1960s, outlasting revenue steam on virtually all other North American Class 1 railroads. *John Gruber*

PLATE 98

A view from the caboose shows Rio Grande K-37 Mikado No. 493 leading one of the railroad's revenue narrow-gauge freights. *John Gruber*

PLATE 99

San Luis Central No. 1 (known as Little Nell) was a 2-8-0 purchased new from Baldwin. It arrived in Monte Vista late in January 1914. San Luis Central carefully maintained the engine, which was the only steam locomotive ever owned by the railroad. Sadly, it was scrapped in 1955. This photo appears in *The Age of Steam: A Classic Album of American Railroading* (1957) with the comment that SLC trains "are so infrequent that local legend holds they are only accomplished in the dark of the moon." The authors, Lucius Beebe and Charles Clegg, were not successful in their quest for a photo, but Gordon Crowell was there at the right time. *Gordon S. Crowell*

PLATES 100 AND 101

Sherman Hill is Union Pacific's big climb west out of Cheyenne. While not as long or as steep as many western graded main lines, it still presented a stiff challenge for freights. UP's 4-8-8-4 Big Boy type was an expansion of its 4-6-6-4 Challenger. Where the Challengers were designed to operate across the UP, the Big Boy was designed specifically to move heavy freight from Cheyenne to Ogden, Utah.

Jim Shaughnessy recalled his visit to Sherman Hill, where he made these coming and going views of No. 4018 hard at work: "I rode the *Denver Zephyr* to Denver, where I had a friend. He lent me his car for the day, so I made a trip up to Sherman Hill. There were remarkable roads there and I found I could drive the car right to this spot on the hill." Today, No. 4018 is displayed at the Museum of the American Railroad in Frisco, Texas. *Both Jim Shaughnessy*

PLATE 102

Jim Shaughnessy made the most of this day trip from Denver to Union Pacific's main line across Wyoming, capturing these two Big Boys at rest. "I spent the day on Sherman making action photos, then went down to Laramie for some night work," he says. "I'd found that an engine terminal was like a theatrical performance. I worked with a Graphic Flash Gun with No. 25 bulbs. Unlike today's electronic flash, each bulb gave me just one flash. For night shots I'd use my four-by-five camera, which I found easier to keep the shutter open.

"It helped to have an assistant, but at Laramie I was on my own. I had to make the most from each bulb while watching the ambient light to make sure it didn't burn out [overexpose] the photo. I used one flashbulb on each engine. I only had time to make this one exposure, and I wouldn't know until I got home and processed the film if I got it or not." *Jim Shaughnessy*

PLATE 103

Union Pacific's double-track transcontinental main line was a favorite for photographers because of its volume and variety. Except for a nominal grade over Archer Hill, the route followed a low-grade profile east of Cheyenne. For many miles U.S. Highway 30 followed the line, and driving along, a photographer needed to keep an eye to the horizon and watch for the telltale signs of smoke or a headlight that would signify an oncoming train. Catching a Challenger like this at work was a treat, but not all that unusual. *John E. Pickett*

PLATE 104

Great Western Railway is a sugar-hauling short line famous for its late-era steam operations. Engine No. 90, a 2-10-2, was preserved and today regularly works on Pennsylvania's Strasburg Railroad. *John E. Pickett*

PLATE 105

By the early 1950s, most American railroads were working with both steam and diesel power. Where some railroads converted whole divisions to diesel operation virtually overnight, other lines took a more gradual approach. Where steam and diesel coexisted, it wasn't uncommon to find steam and diesel locomotives working alongside one another or even together. Yet pictures of steam and diesels together are relatively rare because some photographers would put their cameras down if a diesel was in view. *John E. Pickett*

PLATE 106

Richard Steinheimer was among the most gifted photographers working in the West—or all of the United States, for that matter—during the steam-to-diesel transition. His eye for detail and light combined with an understanding of railroading to produce thousands of stunning images. His notes on this photograph reads: "Example of two different generations of passenger engines; Santa Fe steam loco No. 3753 4-8-4 and new diesel loco in foreground in from Los Angeles with passengers milling around. View from south wing of the San Diego Depot, August 1949."

Originally exposed on color film, this image was converted to black-and-white as a means to compensate for badly shifted colors. *Richard Steinheimer*

PLATE 107

John Pickett made this classic profile of a Northern Pacific Ten-Wheeler on an epic thirty-five-day trip photographing steam locomotives in 1955. "I was traveling with Ray Buhrmaster, Bruce Black, and Dave Bartlett," he recalls. "We spent a total of three nights in motels. Instead we'd sleep in the car and take in roadhouses along the way. I was driving my 1952 Mercury hardtop sedan. What great a trip. We spent several days with the Northern Pacific . . . one of my favorite roads." *John E. Pickett*

PLATE 108

After steam finished in the United States and Canada, photographers looked south of the border where a variety of steam—most of it from American builders Alco and Baldwin—still worked. John spent several productive days with a group of photographers in spring 1961 making photos on Mexican railways. Clear days and open desert country provided excellent conditions to capture steam at work. *John E. Pickett*

PLATE 109

Richard Steinheimer made numerous trips to photograph the West Side Lumber Company's narrow-gauge railway in the final three years of its operation. The line closed for revenue traffic in autumn 1960 and was abandoned in 1961. It was considered the last of the three-foot-gauge lumber railways in the American West. Like many lumber company railroads, it employed Shay and Heisler steam locomotives. These geared engines offered great tractive effort at slow speeds and were designed to negotiate cheaply built track with steep gradients and sharp curves. The end of steam also spelled the end of the line. Steinheimer used flashbulbs to illuminate these Sierra foothills scenes. *Richard Steinheimer*

PLATE 110

In the late 1920s, Southern Pacific completed a shortcut for freight by melding existing lines with new construction. Variously known as the Alturas Cutoff or the Modoc Line, this was among the most remote heavy railway lines in the United States. It connected with SP's primary east–west Overland Route main line at Fernley, Nevada, and continued over a Sawtooth profile through barren high desert across northern California via Wendel and Alturas to connect with SP's Cascade Route at Klamath Falls, Oregon. Southern Pacific regularly operated its large articulated steam locomotives here later than it did on many other lines, and in the mid-1950s photographers made the long trek into remote desert regions to capture them on film. In this view at the Fernley wye, Richard Steinheimer captured a classic view of a locomotive and its crew. It is believed the engine may have been running light from Southern Pacific's yard at Sparks, Nevada (near the base of Donner Pass), to Wendel, where helpers were typically added to Oregon-bound Modoc trains. *Richard Steinheimer*

PLATE 111

During John Pickett's big 1955 trip across the West, he and his friends chased this train on the Modoc Line. At one point the train stopped and the crew offered some of them a cab ride. This image was probably exposed during their chase near where it ran along Pyramid Lake. In 1964, Southern Pacific abandoned the Modoc line south of Wendel, California, between Flanigan and Fernley, Nevada, and secured trackage rights over the roughly parallel Western Pacific main line to Winnemucca, Nevada. *John E. Pickett*

PLATE 112

Where Southern Pacific had been mostly steam-powered at the end of World War II, by the mid-1950s steam was thin on the ground. The final standard-gauge runs came in 1957. This 4-8-2 Mountain type was built at the railroads shops in Sacramento. *Fred Matthews*

PLATE 113

Southern Pacific's streamlined Daylights were some of the flashiest trains in the West. Every day *Morning Daylight* trains 98 and 99 left San Francisco and Los Angeles, respectively, for their sprints along the coast. For these runs, Southern Pacific looked to Lima for some of the finest locomotives ever to work Western rails. John Pickett caught this GS-4 4-8-4 on an August morning at Bayshore Yard. *John E. Pickett*

PLATE 114

As diesels were assigned to work Southern Pacific's premier passenger trains, many large engines were left surplus for other tasks. Where a few years earlier this former *Daylight*-painted 4-8-4 GS-4 would have been assigned long-distance trains like the *Morning Daylight* or *The Lark*, it has been dressed in black for demotion to work the San Francisco–San Jose "Commutes." One of Southern Pacific's last big steam shows was the Commute rushes to and from San Francisco. "This was an early morning run, as some of the midday trains began getting diesels from about 1953," Fred Matthews says of this image. "There had been a gradual progression from older to new steam locomotives showing up on Commutes. This photo was made right at the end of steam and was the last hurrah for SP's steam power." *Fred Matthews*

PLATE 115

In the 1940s, Jack London Square was a busy industrial area near the Oakland waterfront. A large crowd has gathered to board Southern Pacific's special. The locomotive hauling it is a rather elderly heavy 4-6-0 (built by Baldwin in 1912), yet it is sufficient power for the train. It was destined for Stanford at Palo Alto and may have gone via the Dumbarton Bridge that crossed the lower reaches of San Francisco Bay. *Fred Matthews*

PLATE 116

In 1953, Robert Buck and Warren St. George were on a cross-country train trip. Among the trains they rode was Southern Pacific's famed *Morning Daylight* with a big Lima 4-8-4 in the lead. Bob exposed this photo as the train overtook a perishables freight on the Coast Line with AC-10 cab-forward articulated No. 4222 in the lead. After they passed, the freight lined out on the main line and followed the train toward Los Angeles. *Robert A. Buck*

PLATE 117

Fred Matthews and his friends arrived at Dunsmuir on the diesel-hauled *Shasta Daylight* (at right). "We'd come up [from the Bay Area] to ride SP's local to Grants Pass [train 328] on the Siskiyou Line," he recalls, "which was expected to disappear a month later. Dunsmuir was a typical railroad division point with lots of activity and steam locomotive facilities." The Grants Pass local is adjacent to the *Shasta Daylight*. Notice the railroad houses up on the hill. *Fred Matthews*

PLATE 118

Steinheimer's friend, Tom Braunger, watches his engineer father board this cab-forward articulated Class AC-11 at Colton. Southern Pacific bought its first Mallet articulators in 1909 with a conventional cab arrangement. But during operations through the long snow sheds and tunnels on Donner Pass, crews nearly asphyxiated when exhaust fumes filled the cabs. To solve this problem and still take advantage of the superior pulling power of the Mallet compound type, Southern Pacific turned the Mallets around and ran them "cab forward." This was possible because the locomotives were oil-fired. While early cab-forwards were compounds, later machines, like that pictured here, were simple articulated types where high-pressure steam fed all four cylinders directly from the boiler. *Richard Steinheimer*

PLATE 119

This striking nocturnal view was made using a long time exposure mixed with a flashbulb on the front of the cab-forward locomotive. Instead of lighting the side of the train, Richard Steinheimer cross-lit the front and let the side remain dark, allowing for the ghostly, indistinct silhouettes of people on the platform. Glendale was a suburban Los Angeles station used by many long-distance passenger trains. *Richard Steinheimer*

PLATE 120

At the time of this photograph, Jim Shaughnessy was in the National Guard. "I'd be up at Camp Drum [now Fort Drum], New York, and I'd head across the St. Lawrence to Brockville, Ontario, on Canadian National," he recalls. "This was a crew change and a wonderful place to make railroad photographs. No one bothered you and there was lots of activity. Engine 6258 had an unusual front number plate. It was stopped in the yard, and I used two or three bulbs to light it. I found that backlit flash really accentuated details on the locomotive. This is one of my favorite photos." *Jim Shaughnessy*

PLATE 121

Canadian National referred to its 4-8-4s as Confederation types instead of the more common Northern moniker. Canadian National, with its American subsidiary Grand Trunk Western, had the largest roster of 4-8-4s in North America at 203 locomotives. These were dual-service machines and relatively lightweight compared to those used on most U.S. railways, which allowed them greater route availability. *J. William Vigrass*

PLATE 122

The agile, lightweight 4-4-0s were well-suited to branch lines with limited axle weight. A handful of ancient 4-4-0s survived in daily revenue service on the Canadian Pacific until the end of steam. This was an unusually late date to find a 4-4-0 in action *George C. Corey*

PLATE 123

At first glance this might appear to be an ordinary engine leading a passenger train. In fact, it is a rare photo of one of two Canadian Pacific 4-8-4s. Where Canadian National preferred the 4-8-4 design for its late-era steam, Canadian Pacific largely opted for six-coupled designs, notably its famous 4-6-4 Hudsons. Its two 4-8-4s were normally assigned to heavy sleeping-car trains between Montreal and Toronto. When these were displaced by new diesels, however, it allowed for unusual opportunities to see them on daylight runs elsewhere. *Jim Shaughnessy*

PLATES 124 AND 125

These coming and going views show one of Canadian Pacific's once-common Pacific types at work with a holiday special in Montreal at the tail end of the road's steam operations. The Budd RDCs show the great contrast between new and old at the time of the steam-to-diesel transition. This engine holds a special place for Ron Wright. "I have both builder's plates from that engine," he says. *Both Ron Wright*

PLATE 126

No. 1083 was a Class D10 4-6-0 built in the early twentieth century and one of hundreds of Ten-Wheelers that worked across the Canadian Pacific's transcontinental system. This view gives good details of the marker lights, headlight, and number plate. The engine had just worked a snowplow extra. *Ron Wright*

PLATE 127

Ron Wright made this study of the machinery on No. 5107 at the Megantic, Quebec, roundhouse. They had arrived at Megantic the night before by train after an exhausting day of photography in subzero temperatures. Ron explains that this 2-8-2 had brought the Canadian Pacific Scoot into town. *Ron Wright*

PLATE 128

Jim Shaughnessy made the most of a common scene, choosing a dramatic angle that accentuated the power of the locomotive while using the geometry of the crossing to focus interest on the train, all without deemphasizing its environment. *Jim Shaughnessy*

PLATE 129

Jim Shaughnessy was visiting his friend Sandy "S.S." Worthen in Montreal when they made images of this 2-10-2 working freight transfer runs to and from Canadian National's sprawling Turcot Yard. CN favored Elesco feedwater heaters on its late-era locomotives. This external appliance improved an engine's thermal efficiency by using recirculated exhaust gases to prewarm water before it was introduced to the boiler. Some railroads disguised feedwater heaters with jacketing, but CN hung them above the headlight, giving locomotives a "beetle-brow" appearance. *Jim Shaughnessy*

PLATE 130

This broadside image was made on a fine spring day in the Chaurdière River Valley as the train was working north from the U.S.-Canada border at Lac Frontiere toward Vallée Jonction. Jim Shaugnessy, who was traveling with John Pickett, recalls, "On those trips, John would fly to Burlington, Vermont, and then we'd continue to Quebec." On this morning, they knew the train in question was already on the road, "So we drove out of town against the train to intercept it," Jim explains. *Jim Shaughnessy*

PLATE 131

On other days this schedule might have been filled with Budd RDCs, but to accommodate the swell of holiday traffic, it ran as a longer consist with a traditional locomotive—in this case a 2-8-2 Mikado—and cars. Ron Wright still feels a chill when he looks at this image: "Boy it was cold! Bitter." *Ron Wright*

PLATE 132

The Quebec Central was a Canadian Pacific subsidiary connecting Quebec City with Newport, Vermont, plus branches to Megantic (where it met Canadian Pacific's east–west main line from Montreal to St. John, New Brunswick), and from Vallée Jonction to Lac Frontiere. The train pictured was one of three plough extras working out of the Vallée Jonction yard on the last day of 1959. This relatively remote location was a holdout for Canadian Pacific steam in its final months of service. In eastern Canada, the railroad's revenue steam was effectively finished by April 1960, although some engines were retained a while longer for standby service. *Ron Wright*

PLATE 133

Located near the border with Maine, Megantic, Quebec, was a crew change and the location of a small yard. In 2013, more than fifty-three years after this image was exposed, Megantic was the site of one of Canada's worst railway disasters. *Ron Wright*

PLATE 134

As diesels took over, American railroads scrapped thousands of steam locomotives like these awaiting a date with the cutting torch. For the enthusiast, the curtain was falling on the great show. Southern Pacific's Bayshore Yard was located on filled land immediately south of San Francisco on the Harriman-era Bayshore cutoff. *Richard Steinheimer*

SELECT BIBLIOGRAPHY

BOOKS

Alexander, Edwin P. *American Locomotives*. New York: Bonza Books, 1950.

———. *Iron Horses*. New York: Bonza Books, 1941.

Brown, John K. *The Baldwin Locomotive Works 1831–1915*. Baltimore: The Johns Hopkins University Press, 1995.

Bruce, Alfred W. *The Steam Locomotive in America*. New York: Norton, 1952.

Churella, Albert J. *From Steam to Diesel*. Princeton, N.J.: Princeton University Press, 1998.

Conrad, J. David. *The Steam Locomotive Directory of North America*. 2 vols. Polo, Ill.: Transportation Trails, 1988.

Drury, George H. *Guide to North American Steam Locomotives*. Waukesha, Wis.: Kalmbach Publishing, 1993.

———. *The Historical Guide to North American Railroads*. Waukesha, Wis.: Kalmbach Publishing, 1985.

Dunscomb, Guy, L. *A Century of Southern Pacific Steam Locomotives*. Modesto, Calif.: Guy L. Dunscomb & Son, 1963.

Encyclopedia of American Business History and Biography: Railroads in the Nineteenth Century. New York: Bruccoli Clark Layman and Facts on File, 1988.

Farrington, S. Kip Jr. *Railroading from the Head End*. New York: Doubleday, Doran & Co., 1943.

———. *Railroading from the Rear End*. New York: Doubleday, Doran & Co., 1946.

———. *Railroading the Modern Way*. New York: Doubleday, Doran & Co., 1951.

———. *Railroads at War*. New York: Doubleday, Doran & Co., 1944.

———. *Railroads of Today*. New York: Doubleday, Doran & Co., 1949.

Frey, Robert L. *Railroads in the Nineteenth Century*. New York: Facts on File, 1988.

Garmany, John B. *Southern Pacific Dieselization*. Edmonds, Wash.: Pacific Fast Mail, 1985.

Gruber, John. *Railroad History in a Nutshell*. Madison, Wis.: Center for Railroad Photography and Art, 2009.

———. *Railroad Preservation in a Nutshell*. Madison, Wis.: Center for Railroad Photography and Art, 2011.

Hampton, Taylor. *The Nickel Plate Road*. Cleveland, Ohio: World Publishing, 1947.

Hilton, George W. *American Narrow Gauge Railroads*. Stanford, Calif.: Stanford University Press, 1990.

Holton, James L. *The Reading Railroad: History of a Coal Age Empire*. 2 vols. Laurys Station, Penn.: Garrigues House, 1992.

Kiefer, P. W. *A Practical Evaluation of Railroad Motive Power*. New York: Simmons-Boardman, 1948.

Kirkland, John, F. *Dawn of the Diesel Age*. Pasadena, Calif.: Interurban Press, 1994.

Klein, Maury. *History of the Louisville & Nashville Railroad*. New York: Macmillan, 1972.

———. *Union Pacific*. 2 vols. New York: Doubleday, 1989.

Kratville, William, and Harold E. Ranks. *Motive Power of the Union Pacific*. Omaha, Neb.: Kratville Publishing, 1958.

LeMassena, Robert A. *Colorado's Mountain Railroads*. Golden, Colo.: Sundance Publications, 1963.

———. *Rio Grande to the Pacific*. Denver, Colo.: Sundance Publications, 1974.

Middleton, William D., with George M. Smerk and Roberta L. Diehl. *Encyclopedia of North American Railroads*. Bloomington, Ind.: Indiana University Press, 2007.

Morgan, David P. *Steam's Finest Hour*. Milwaukee, Wis.: Kalmbach Publishing, 1959.

Ransome-Wallis, P. *The Concise Encyclopedia of World Railway Locomotives*. New York: Hawthorn Books, 1959.

Reck, Franklin M. *On Time*. LaGrange, Ill.: Electro-Motive Division of General Motors, 1948.

Schafer, Mike, and Brian Solomon. *Pennsylvania Railroad*. Minneapolis, Minn: Voyageur Press, 2009.

Shaughnessy, Jim. *Delaware & Hudson*. Berkeley, Calif.: Howell North Books, 1967.

———. *The Rutland Road, 2nd Ed.* Syracuse, N.Y.: Howell-North, 1997.

Signor, John R. *Beaumont Hill*. San Marino, Calif.: Golden West Books, 1990.

———. *Donner Pass: Southern Pacific's Sierra Crossing*. San Marino, Calif.: Golden West Books, 1985.

Sinclair, Angus. *Development of the Locomotive Engine*. New York: A. Sinclair Publishing, 1907.

Smith, Warren L. *Berkshire Days on the Boston & Albany*. New York: Quadrant Press, 1982.

Solomon, Brian. *Alco Locomotives*. Minneapolis, Minn.: Voyageur Press, 2009.

———. *The American Steam Locomotive*. Osceola, Wis.: Motorbooks, 1998.

———. *Baldwin Locomotives*. Minneapolis, Minn.: Voyageur Press, 2010.

———. *Locomotive*. Osceola, Wis.: MBI Publishing Company, 2001.

———. *Railroads of Pennsylvania*. Minneapolis, Minn.: Voyageur Press, 2008.

———. *Southern Pacific Passenger Trains*. St. Paul, Minn.: MBI Publishing Company, 2005.

———. *Super Steam Locomotives*. Osceola, Wis.: MBI Publishing Co., 2000.

Solomon, Brian, and Mike Schafer. *New York Central Railroad*. Osceola, Wis.: MBI Publishing Company, 1999.

Staufer, Alvin F. *C&O Power*. Carrollton, Ohio: A. F. Staufer, 1965.

———. *Pennsy Power III*. Medina, Ohio: A. F. Staufer, 1993.

———. *Steam Power of the New York Central System, Vol. 1*. Medina, Ohio: A. F. Staufer, 1961.

Staufer, Alvin F., and Edward L. May. *New York Central's Later Power*. Medina, Ohio: A. F. Staufer, 1981.

Steinbrenner, Richard T. *The American Locomotive Company: A Centennial Remembrance*. Warren, N.J.: On Track Publishers, 2003.

Stover, John F. *History of the New York Central Railroad*. New York: Macmillan, 1975.

———. *The Life and Decline of the American Railroad*, New York: Oxford University Press, 1970.

———. *The Routledge Historical Atlas of the American Railroads*. New York: Routledge, 1999.

Swengel, Frank M. *The American Steam Locomotive: Vol. 1, Evolution*. Davenport, Iowa: Midwest Rail Publications, 1967.

Westing, Frederic, and Alvin F. Staufer. *Erie Power*. Medina, Ohio: Wayner, 1970.

White, John H. Jr., *A History of the American Locomotive: Its Development, 1830–1880*. Baltimore: Dover, 1968.

Wilson, O. Meredith. *The Denver and Rio Grande Project, 1870–1901*. Salt Lake City, Utah: Howe Brothers, 1982.

Winchester, Clarence. *Railway Wonders of the World*, 2 vols. London: Amalgamated Press, 1935.

Wright, Richard K. *Southern Pacific Daylight*. Thousand Oaks, Calif.: RKW Publication, 1970.

PERIODICALS

Baldwin Locomotives. Philadelphia (no longer published)

The Car and Locomotive Cyclopedia, Omaha, Neb.

Classic Trains, Waukesha, Wis.

Locomotive Cyclopedia, New York, 1922–1947 (no longer published)

Official Guide to the Railways, New York

Railroad History, formerly *Railway and Locomotive Historical Society Bulletin*, Boston

Railway Age, Chicago and New York

Railway and Locomotive Engineering, New York (no longer published)

Railway Gazette, New York, 1870–1908 (no longer published)

The Railway Gazette, London

Railway Mechanical Engineer, 1925–1952 (no longer published)

Trains, Waukesha, Wis.

Vintage Rails, Waukesha, Wis. (no longer published)

ACKNOWLEDGMENTS

CREDIT FOR THIS BOOK goes first and foremost to the photographers who made the images that appear on the preceding pages. These men shared a passion for the railroad and its locomotives, and from an early age learned to translate their interest into graphic images that have withstood the test of time.

What is remarkable is that most of the photographers featured were in their teens when they began making images. It's because of their farsighted vision that this book was possible. It takes a talented personality to successfully combine a working knowledge of railway operations with an understanding of light and photographic technique to be able to repeatedly execute stunning railway images. Add to that talent the foresight to recognize that the machines that had ruled the rails for a century would soon all but disappear, and to act on that intuition despite obligations of family, school, military service, and employment, often while working with very limited budgets. It should be of little surprise that many of the photographers featured developed careers as either professional image-makers or railroaders, translating their passion into a livelihood. Each photographer is credited with his images.

Although too often they go nameless, thanks is owed to the railroaders, many tacit enthusiasts themselves, who facilitated the image-making process. Without them there would be no smoke, steam, or trains behind the engines. Especially important were the many friendly railroaders who helped photographers by offering visits to roundhouses, engine rides, location suggestions, vital information on train operations, and warnings about pending changes.

I could not have produced this work without the help of many people, including most of the photographers themselves, who assisted with telling me the details of their experiences, often as long as six decades after the images were made. John Gruber was invaluable. Not only did he lend some of his photographs and recollections, he provided information on the work of Richard Steinheimer and Gordon S. Crowell and introduced me to Philip A. Weibler. Thanks to Shirley Burman, Richard Steinheimer's widow, who graciously supplied photographs and recollections. Pat Yough assisted with Gordon R. Roth's work, introduced me to Ronald Wright, and provided transport on several occasions. Eric M. Johnson supplied location information for Elmira Branch images. Special thanks to John E. Pickett and Jim Shaughnessy, both of whom I've interviewed on several occasions. Fred Matthews provided an appreciation and understanding of the Southern Pacific that transcends his gorgeous photographs; likewise Bill Vigrass gave me a better appreciation for the Erie and the Nickel Plate Road. Paul Carver, George C. Corey, and the late Robert A. Buck tutored me on the finer points of steam locomotives on many occasions. Both George and Bob have photos in these pages.

My editor, Dennis Pernu, helped refine the concept for the book as well as the text. Although he has no photographs in this book, my father, Richard J. Solomon, spent his early years photographing railways intensely and passed that interest on to me. Interestingly, his early work is almost exclusively color, which is out of the realm of this book, but has appeared in my other published works. Thanks to the Irish Railway Record Society for the use of its library and to its members for detailed discussions of railway and locomotive operations.

In the text and captions, I've tried to provide some insight into the stories and techniques behind many of the images. Basic captions appear with each photograph, while more detailed captions are located toward the back of the book. Working from many sources, I've gone to great lengths to procure accurate and interesting information; however, if mistakes occur, they are mine and not those of the folks who helped me. No author is perfect and no book final.

First published in 2014 by Voyageur Press, a member of Quayside Publishing Group Inc., 400 First Avenue North, Suite 400, Minneapolis, MN 55401 USA

© 2014 Voyageur Press

Photography © 2014 Family of Robert A. Buck, Shirley Burman, George C. Corey, Gordon S. Crowell, John Gruber, Fred Matthews, Bob Meiborg, John E. Pickett, Gordon R. Roth, Jim Shaughnessy, J. William Vigrass, Philip A. Weibler, Ron Wright, and Richard H. Young

Voyageur Press titles are also available at discounts in bulk quantity for industrial or sales-promotional use.
For details write to Special Sales Manager at Quayside Publishing Group Inc., 400 First Avenue North, Suite 400, Minneapolis, MN 55401 USA.

To find out more about our books, visit us online at www.voyageurpress.com.

ISBN: 0-7603-978-4586-3

Library of Congress Cataloging-in-Publication Data
Solomon, Brian, 1966-
The twilight of steam : great photography from the last days
of steam locomotives in America / Brian Solomon.
pages cm
Includes bibliographical references and index.
ISBN 978-0-7603-4586-3 (hc)
1. Steam locomotives--United States--History. 2. Steam locomotives--United States--Pictorial works. 3.
Steam locomotives--Canada--History. 4. Steam locomotives--Canada--Pictorial works. I. Title.
TJ603.2.S66 2014
625.26'1097309045--dc23
2013044102

Design Manager: James Kegley
Cover Designer: Kent Jenson
Layout Designer: Chris Fayers

Printed in China

10 9 8 7 6 5 4 3 2 1

PLATE 134 (FOLLOWING PAGE): Bayshore Yard, South San Francisco, February 1, 1957. *Richard Steinheimer*
COVER: Illinois Central's Paducah, Kentucky, yard, September 1, 1957. *Jim Shaughnessy*
BACK COVER: Denver & Rio Grande Western's Farmington Branch, 1967. John Gruber